WILLIAMS-SONOMA

MASTERING

Vegetables

General Editor
CHUCK WILLIAMS

Recipes
DEBORAH MADISON

Photographs
TUCKER & HOSSLER

NEW YORK · LONDON · TORONTO · SYDNEY

7 About This Book

8 Working with the Recipes

9 Types of Vegetables

12 Cooking with the Seasons

14 Cooking, Seasoning & Serving Vegetables

18 Basic Recipes

20 Basic Steamed Vegetables

22 Basic Braised Vegetables

24 Basic Sautéed Vegetables

26 Basic Roasted Vegetables

28 Key Techniques

30 Dicing an Onion

31 Dicing a Shallot

32 Working with Garlic

33 Working with Green Onions and Jalapeño Chiles

34 Working with Herbs

36 Toasting Nuts & Seeds

37 Making Fresh Bread Crumbs and Dicing Bacon

38 Zesting & Juicing Citrus and Trimming Broccoli

39 Trimming Cauliflower and Working with Cabbage

40 Stemming & Rinsing Greens and Working with Fennel

42 Preparing Brussels Sprouts and Working with Round Vegetables

43 Preparing Winter Squash and Fresh Mushrooms

Contents

44 Steamed & Boiled Vegetables

47 **Classic Mashed Potatoes** *master recipe

52 Mashed Potato Variations

54 Steamed Broccoli with Lemon & Olive Oil

56 Steamed Vegetable Variations

59 Green Beans & Yellow Wax Beans with Pesto

60 Corn on the Cob with Chile-Lime Butter

62 Braised Vegetables

65 **Braised Artichokes with Shallots & Peas** *master recipe

70 Braised Fennel with White Wine & Tomato

73 Braised Vegetable Variations

75 Maple-Glazed Carrots with Shallots & Parsley

77 Glazed Vegetable Variations

79 Quick Braise of Spring Peas with Red Onion Shoots

80 Red Cabbage Braised with Bacon & Apples

83 Braised Mushrooms with Sherry & Cream

84 Braised Brussels Sprouts with Bacon & Onion

86 Sautéed & Stir-fried Vegetables

89 **Stir-fried Spring Vegetables with Ginger, Lemon & Mint** *master recipe

95 Sautéed Peppers & Onion

97 Sautéed Vegetable Variations

98 Sautéed Spinach with Garlic & Lemon

100 Sautéed Green Variations

103 Stir-fried Sesame Eggplant

104 Roasted & Baked Vegetables

107 **Tomatoes Stuffed with Rice, Basil & Cheese** *master recipe

113 **Roasted Winter Root Vegetables with Rosemary** *master recipe

118 Roasted Vegetable Variations

121 **Summer Squash Tian** *master recipe

126 Classic Potato Gratin

129 Gratin Variations

131 Roasted Asparagus with Orange-Shallot Butter

132 Using Key Tools & Equipment

136 Glossary

140 Index

144 Acknowledgments

About this book

Mastering Vegetables offers every reader a cooking class in book form, a one-on-one lesson with a seasoned teacher standing by your side explaining each recipe step-by-step—with plenty of photographs to illustrate every detail.

Vegetables arguably offer more diversity than any other category of ingredients in the kitchen. They promise a range of colors and textures—think of bright red, crisp sautéed bell peppers; pale gold, fluffy mashed Yukon gold potatoes; and deep green, tender roasted asparagus. And, they can be prepared by nearly every cooking method—steaming, boiling, braising, sautéing, stir-frying, roasting, and baking. Many people rely on the same method and seasoning whenever they prepare vegetables. Too often that means boiled and topped with a pat of butter. But cooking them is much more than that simple formula!

Here's how this book covers a complete beginning course on vegetables: The introduction describes dozens of different varieties and their seasons, and offers guidelines on how to cook them. Next, the Basic Recipes chapter includes recipes for the four most common ways to cook vegetables: steaming, braising, sautéing, and roasting. Then, the Key Techniques chapter teaches you, through both photographs and instructive text, the essential skills needed to prepare common ingredients, from how to dice a shallot to how to trim a cauliflower or zest a lemon. Finally, the recipe chapters, which build on the classic techniques you've already learned, will let you put your newfound knowledge to work at the stove. You'll find chapters devoted to steaming and boiling; braising; sautéing and stir-frying; and roasting and baking.

Once you have mastered the recipes in this book, you will find yourself adding the bright flavor of vegetables to every meal you prepare.

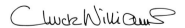

Working with the Recipes

Everyone knows how important it is to eat plenty of vegetables to ensure a healthful lifestyle. But while you may be familiar with such common varieties as carrots and corn, tomatoes and potatoes, you may not know as much about other types or how to cook them. This book will teach you about many of these lesser-known vegetables, now available in supermarkets and farmers' markets, and the cooking methods that show them to their best advantage.

The recipes in this book build on one another to give you a sound introduction to a wide variety of vegetables and the best ways to cook them. The four recipe chapters are organized by the classic cooking techniques you will use. The first chapter focuses on two basic moist-heat methods, steaming and boiling, while the second chapter concentrates on braising, another moist-heat method. Next come the quick techniques of sautéing and stir-frying, followed by two dry-heat methods, roasting and baking.

Master recipes at the beginning of each chapter ground you in these various techniques. These recipes will take you through each cooking stage, step-by-step, as if you had a cooking teacher instructing you as you work. And remember, the more you practice, the better prepared you'll be the next time. After sharpening your skills in the master recipes, try some of the other, less-detailed recipes in each chapter. They will give you the chance to practice your new skills and build your confidence gradually.

Each chapter also includes recipe variations that utilize some of the same techniques you have already learned, but with different ingredients. For example, after you have mastered how to make Steamed Broccoli with Lemon & Olive Oil (page 54), you will have the know-how to prepare Cauliflower with Curry Butter (page 56).

For more information on the types of pots, pans, steamers, and other basic equipment you will need to get started cooking vegetables, turn to page 132.

Types of Vegetables

Vegetables can be grouped by various defining elements. Some groups are botanically based, such as leeks, onions, garlic, and chives, all of which belong to the *Allium* genus. Botanically related vegetables often share similar flavors or shapes. Other groups are made up of botanically unrelated members with common characteristics, such as leafy greens, which include examples from a number of genera. Both types of groupings are represented here.

Here's a brief look at some vegetable groups, their shared characteristics, and how their members are best prepared. The following descriptions include only the vegetables found in this book.

Leafy Greens

This group includes spinach, kale, collard greens, chard, and broccoli rabe. All leafy greens cook in a relatively short amount of time, from just a few minutes, in the case of spinach, to as many as seven or more, in the case of collards and kale. And all leafy greens diminish significantly in volume when cooked. A hefty bunch of spinach or stemmed chard leaves will shrink to a small bowlful when cooked. Kale, collards, and broccoli rabe retain a bit more volume, as does Belgian endive (chicory/witloof).

While Brussels sprouts and cabbage are not generally thought of or treated as greens, when the leaves are separated, they can be sautéed or stir-fried in the same manner as greens. Loose leafy greens are often cultivated in sandy soil, so take extra care when rinsing them before cooking. Always give spinach at least two good rinses in a large basin of water before preparing.

Brassicas (Cabbages and Relatives)

This group, which includes not only cabbages of all kinds but also broccoli, cauliflower, Brussels sprouts, and other similarly dense vegetables, is part of the large mustard family. Bok choy and napa cabbage are two well-known Asian members, but there are scores more. Often described as dietary weapons in the fight against cancer, brassicas are among the most important vegetables to eat for ensuring a regimen rich in antioxidants, vitamin C, and fiber.

There's no reason to fear this group's reputation for being strong tasting. The flavor is mostly a result of how you cook them. Steaming is a good method, or boiling in salted water, but what's most important is not to overcook them. Although they look solid and sturdy, it is possible to cook them to mush, at which point they will have lost their appeal.

Roots & Tubers

This potpourri includes vegetables that grow underground: carrots, potatoes, turnips, rutabagas, celery root (celeriac), sweet potatoes, beets, and others. Even though they come from different botanical genera, they all tend to be sweet and dense, and they typically take more time to cook than other vegetables.

These solid vegetables can be steamed, boiled, and even braised. They don't lend themselves to sautéing, though, unless

they are either partially cooked or thinly sliced. Roasting, however, is a particularly good method because it both brings out their sugars and cooks off their moisture to intensify their flavors. Many roots and tubers have a natural flavor affinity for one another: potatoes are a delicious match with turnips and celery root, as you'll see in some of the mashed potato variations on page 53.

Pods & Seeds

Even though corn, peas, and beans look very different, they are among the vegetables whose seeds we eat. When fresh, all of them cook quickly, needing little more than a brief plunge into boiling water or an equally quick turn in the wok or frying pan. In their dried form, however, these vegetables take hours of simmering to become tender.

Mushrooms

Mushrooms make up a category all their own, but many different varieties are found within it. The most common members are cultivated, including white, cremini (also called baby bellas), portobello (which are simply large cremini), shiitake, and oyster. The first three have a similar, mild woodsy flavor. Shiitake mushrooms are stronger flavored, while mild-tasting oyster mushrooms, which look like velvet, cook more quickly than the others and are often added toward the end of a recipe. Wild mushrooms, such as chanterelle, morel, and porcini, have marvelous, distinctive flavors and appearances that set them apart from their cultivated counterparts. They are also more costly and only seasonally available.

All mushrooms cook relatively quickly, which makes them good candidates for sautéing, stir-frying, or brief braising. Mushrooms are usually not steamed or boiled, which can cause them to become unpleasantly waterlogged.

Vegetable Fruits

Botanically, eggplants (aubergines), tomatoes, bell peppers (capsicums), and chiles are fruits, not vegetables, but since we treat them like vegetables, they have been dubbed vegetable fruits to acknowledge their dual personalities. They are all harvested in the summer, and with the exception of eggplants, we often, though certainly not always, discard their seeds before eating them. Juicy and flavorful, these vegetables are good subjected to the high heat of sautéing or stir-frying, but they also respond well to braising, where they release their natural sweetness.

Organic Vegetables

The vegetables we're encouraged to eat because they are packed with nutrients can be loaded with pesticides, too. Broccoli, for example, is one of the most heavily sprayed vegetables, and fiber- and flavor-rich potato skins retain pesticides. Many studies have shown that consuming pesticides is not good for anyone, especially children. And food grown with pesticides harms not only those who eat it, but also those who grow it, the water supply, and the general health of wildlife.

It is not uncommon for people to ask if organic vegetables taste better. Usually they do, but taste depends on many factors, including the variety, when they are harvested, and how far they're shipped, so superior taste is not always guaranteed. But better health for you and the environment is always guaranteed, so choose organically grown or pesticide-free vegetables whenever possible.

Squashes

Whether summer or winter, large or small, or plain or exotic in shape and color, zucchini (courgette), butternut, kabocha, and other squash varieties—of which there are hundreds—are all plants of the gourd family. Summer squashes are characterized by their smooth, tender skin and relatively delicate flesh, while winter squashes are known for their protective hard shell and dense flesh, which make them good keepers over the winter months.

Both summer and winter squashes are tremendously versatile. They can be steamed, boiled, roasted, braised, sautéed, and stir-fried, and they can even take a turn on the grill. They run from fairly bland (summer squash) to quite sweet (winter squash).

Stalks

One of the more unusual categories of vegetable, stalks include such wildly different examples as asparagus, fennel, celery, and even artichokes, which include the flower bud as well as the stem, or stalk. These vegetables have little in common with one another except for their elongated forms. Thick asparagus, fennel, and celery are improved if you peel them, and artichoke stems, when you can find the flower buds with their stems still attached, should be thickly peeled as well.

This group is versatile when it comes to cooking methods. All can be steamed, sautéed, braised—and some, such as asparagus, can be roasted as well—alone or in the company of other vegetables.

Alliums (Onions)

Yellow, white, and red onions; boiling onions; pearl onions; garlic; green (spring) onions; shallots; leeks; and chives are all bulbous members of the large *Allium* genus, which is part of the big lily family. They share similar flavors, even though their shapes and sizes vary widely, and they are often used in dishes in which they do not star: a base of sautéed onions or leeks is the first step for many braises, the addition of garlic can deliver a touch of pungency to a stir-fry or a sauté, and a garnish of slivered green onions or finely snipped chives adds color and flavor to all kinds of dishes. But many alliums are also cooked as vegetables in their own right, such as Leeks with Mustard Sauce (page 73) or Glazed Pearl Onions with Rosemary (page 77).

Cooking with the Seasons

All vegetables have one or more times of the year when they are in season. Artichokes peak in the spring and again at the end of summer. Tomatoes have their moment from midsummer until the first freeze, while spinach and peas thrive in cool weather. Because some varieties, such as carrots, potatoes, and turnips, store well, we associate them with winter. But even these so-called winter vegetables are actually truly fresh in summer and autumn.

Eating seasonally allows us to enjoy vegetables at their peak of flavor and tenderness. But with so many vegetables available year-round these days, true seasonality is often hard to recognize. Most large supermarkets paint a picture of the seasons with such broad strokes that shoppers automatically associate February with artichokes and March with asparagus, even though these vegetables may be months away from being in season locally. To take advantage of the benefits that seasonal vegetables offer, you need to

be in tune with what is growing where you live, or at least nearby. In other words, it is important to eat vegetables both seasonally and locally.

A farmers' market is probably the best place to discover what's in season where you live. For example, summertime means tomatoes, but if you live in a hot, dry, low-lying area, the height of summer may be too hot for tomatoes, while if you live at a northern altitude or a high elevation, tomatoes are likely at their best on the first of September. Of course, no matter

where you live, the broadest definitions of the seasons apply, so that the same foods, such as corn, eggplants, green beans, and peppers, are hot-weather harvests, and asparagus, peas, new potatoes, and green onions are classic cool-weather crops.

Once you begin to eat seasonally, you'll find that the taste you experience can't be beat by produce that's shipped from afar. Freshness has its own flavor, or quality, and the shorter the distance food travels to market, the more it has to offer you.

The seasonal groupings that follow include vegetables as well as the herbs often paired with them. When looking at the groupings, keep in mind that some items appear in more than one season. Carrots arrive in spring and again in late summer, while mushrooms and Belgian endive are year-round. Other varieties, such as beets, store well and can be enjoyed in many seasons.

Spring
Spring signals the end of winter's chill and the promise of warm days to come. Many vegetables, such as peas, are available only for a few weeks early in the season, which runs from April through June, before the weather gets too hot.

artichokes • asparagus • bok choy • carrots
chard • chervil • chives • green (spring) onions
mint • new potatoes • peas (of all kinds)
radishes • spinach • tarragon

Summer
Beginning in July and lasting through September (or until the first freeze), summer is one of the best times to prepare vegetables. These hot months are when most vegetables truly come into season, particularly bright red ones, such as bell peppers and tomatoes. If you live at a high altitude or in a coastal area, peas, fennel, lettuce, and spinach are summer harvests as well.

artichokes (again in September) • basil
beets • bell peppers (capsicums) • broccoli
cabbage • carrots • cauliflower • corn
eggplants (aubergines) • garlic • green beans
marjoram • oregano • summer squashes
tomatoes • turnips

Autumn
This season opens in October and lasts through December, with the days growing shorter and colder as the season progresses. Autumn is a time when many hearty vegetables that were planted during the summer months finish ripening.

Brussels sprouts • cabbage • cauliflower
celery • celery root (celeriac) • fennel • kale
leeks • onions • oregano • rosemary • sage
sweet potatoes • winter squashes

Winter
Winter spans the coldest months of the year, January through March. Many of the vegetables associated with this season have actually been harvested earlier (broccoli, cauliflower, Brussels sprouts, beets, and turnips), but because they are excellent keepers, they are found on the winter table.

beets • broccoli • Brussels sprouts • cabbage
carrots • cauliflower • collards • kale • leeks
onions • potatoes • rutabagas • turnips

Cooking, Seasoning & Serving Vegetables

Preparing any recipe begins with careful planning to ensure that your time at the stove goes smoothly and easily. In this section, you'll learn how to trim and cut up ingredients, how to set up your *mise en place,* how to season vegetables to bring out their natural flavors, and how to keep finished dishes hot during serving. You will also learn about all the ways—from boiling and steaming to baking and roasting—you can cook your favorite vegetables.

Preparing Vegetables

Rinsing, peeling, trimming, and chopping are often the most time-consuming tasks in the preparation of a vegetable dish. But the good news is that the more familiar you become with any vegetable, the faster you will be able to prepare it.

RINSING Most recipes in this book assume that you have rinsed your vegetables before you begin to cut them, a process that both cleans and refreshes them. Some vegetables require special attention, however. Spinach can be sandy and often requires at least two thorough plunges in a large basin of cold water. Soil can lodge in the leaves of leeks, which means they need to be split lengthwise and well rinsed. Celery root can be muddy, so it needs a good rinse and a once-over with a scrub brush. Keep in mind, too, that vegetables you grow yourself or you purchase at a farmers' market might need more rinsing than supermarket produce.

PEELING You need to peel tough outer skins with a vegetable peeler or a paring knife. Broccoli stems are delicious once

their thick, fibrous outer layer is removed, large turnips taste sweeter after they are thickly peeled, and stocky asparagus spears are more succulent without their tough skin. Running a vegetable peeler over celery, fennel, and chard stems rids them of tough strings, while the thin papery skins of onions, shallots, and garlic are always removed.

MISE EN PLACE The term *mise en place*— putting in place—refers to gathering all the elements you need for a recipe before you begin to cook. This includes rinsed, peeled, chopped, minced, and measured ingredients and any equipment you will use. Then, instead of hunting for an ingredient or a utensil when your pan begins to sizzle, whatever you need is within reach.

MEASURING INGREDIENTS Measurements are expressed three ways: weight, number, and volume. Weight is a more reliable measurement than number, making a kitchen scale invaluable. Vegetables vary in size—summer turnips are small, while storage turnips can weigh as much as

½ pound (250 g). That's why you'll see some of the ingredients in this book listed with both number and weight.

Volume measurements are used for dry and liquid ingredients. Measuring cups (usually metal) for dry ingredients are filled level with the rim, while measuring cups for liquids (generally glass with a spout) are filled to the appropriate mark on the side. For accuracy, place a cup with liquid on a flat surface to read the measure at eye level. The same measuring spoons are used for both wet and dry ingredients. This book often calls for ⅛ teaspoon. If you don't have the ⅛-teaspoon measuring spoon, fill the ¼ teaspoon half full.

Chopped herbs and vegetables can be loosely or tightly packed. If a recipe calls for tightly packed ingredients, push them firmly into the measuring cup so little air separates the pieces.

Cooking Vegetables

Vegetables—and the cooking methods used for them—are enormously versatile. They can be steamed and then dressed in an aromatic sauce, sautéed or stir-fried in sizzling oil, braised slowly in stock or wine, or roasted and stuffed and then baked. And regardless of the method, vegetables can be cooked or garnished with bits of bacon, roasted nuts, grated cheese, fresh herbs, or sauces of all kinds.

Some vegetables are better suited to one cooking method than another, while other vegetables can be cooked by nearly any method. And some vegetable dishes may call for two methods: broccoli rabe is sometimes blanched (boiled) first and then sautéed as in Broccoli Rabe with Red Pepper & Garlic (page 100).

BOILING & STEAMING Both of these simple moist-heat methods are a good place for the beginner to start when cooking vegetables. Steaming calls for cooking over a small amount of boiling water, while boiling calls for immersing in a generous amount of boiling water. Today, steaming, in which the vegetables are cooked by the hot rising steam, is the more popular method because it is more efficient and the vegetables' nutrients are not lost in the cooking water.

Most vegetables, including broccoli, corn, new potatoes, winter squashes, bok choy, beets, cabbage, and cauliflower, lend themselves to boiling and steaming. Other vegetables, such as eggplants (aubergines) and mushrooms, do not because they readily absorb the moisture and become soggy.

BRAISING Cooking in a small amount of liquid, or braising, is a slower and gentler moist-heat method than boiling or sautéing. It calls for a heavy pot with a tight-fitting lid so that the liquid can rise as steam, condense on the lid, and then return to moisten and season the vegetable. At the end of cooking, a small amount of well-flavored liquid remains. A braise often combines vegetables, such as Braised Artichokes with Shallots & Peas (page 65), or it results in a sweet glaze coating a single vegetable, such as Mustard-Glazed Parsnips (77).

Knife Safety

A dull knife is more dangerous than a sharp one, so it's important always to keep your knives sharp. When slicing, be sure to curve your fingers away from the blade to avoid cutting yourself. Practice with a knife on scraps, such as the discarded outer leaves of a head of lettuce, to develop ease, speed, and accuracy.

SAUTÉING & STIR-FRYING Both sautéing and stir-frying involve cooking quickly over high heat. The combination of high temperature and hot oil sears vegetables, imparting an appealing flavor. These rapid methods are ideal for menus in which the other dishes can be made ahead.

Traditionally, sautéing is accomplished by jerking the handle of a frying pan so that the ingredients "jump" (the French *sauter* means "to jump") on the hot surface, although you can simply stir the ingredients until you master this technique. For stir-frying, which uses a wok, the vegetables are rapidly tossed with two spoons or spatulas, and a little liquid is often added near the end of cooking to create both steam and a sauce.

BAKING & ROASTING Both of these methods are done in the oven. A baked dish, however, is usually cooked at a temperature of between 350° and 375°F (180° and 190°C), while a roasted dish is usually cooked at 400°F (200°C) or higher. The moderate heat of baking is the ideal way to finish a stuffed vegetable, such as the Tomatoes Stuffed with Rice, Basil & Cheese (page 107), or to cook a gratin of vegetables bound with milk or another liquid, such as Fennel & Potato Gratin (page 129).

Roasted vegetables can be cooked singly, as in Roasted Sweet Potatoes with Soy Glaze (page 119) or in combination, as in Roasted Winter Root Vegetables with Rosemary (page 113). They are usually tossed in oil, which adds flavor and protects them from the drying heat of the oven, and then they are cooked until they lose their moisture, which concentrates their inherent flavors and natural sweetness.

Seasoning Vegetables

A bit of butter or olive oil and a pinch or two of salt and freshly ground pepper makes any simply cooked vegetable taste great, but there's no reason to stop there. Cooked vegetables can be seasoned in many delicious ways.

SALT Salt helps draw out and then build flavors, beginning with the water in which you boil potatoes for mashed potatoes. If you wait until the dish is fully cooked before you add salt, you will be adding only saltiness. But if you taste and season as you go, once you get to the final step, you may need very little salt to sharpen the flavors, or perhaps you will want to add a few drops of lemon juice or vinegar or a bit of pepper instead of salt. That's why some recipes in this book instruct you to taste and adjust the seasonings with salt first. Also, everyone

has a different tolerance for salt and pepper, so tasting is the only way to know how much to add.

BUTTER & OIL Butter is delicious on vegetables and is good in braised dishes, but it can burn at high temperatures, so oil is better for sautéing. Olive oil is a delicious and health-smart choice. For a fruity and flavorful olive oil for cooking, look for moderately priced bottles labeled extra-virgin. For a lighter cooking oil, turn to pure olive oil or a vegetable oil,

Other Flavorings

Pungent mustard is good for balancing sweetness, while vegetables that are not as naturally sweet as they should be benefit from the addition of a little honey. A few drops of soy sauce can provide salt as well as depth of flavor, toasted seeds or nuts can deliver richness and crunch, and capers can wake up a vegetable with their bite. Consider combinations of seasonings, too, such as a sauce of capers, pine nuts, olive oil, and herbs on steamed carrots.

such as canola. Use a more expensive extra-virgin oil for drizzling over a finished dish. Aromatic Asian sesame oil is also a good finishing oil. Drizzle a few drops over steamed vegetables, as in Baby Bok Choy with Sesame Oil (page 56), to enhance a simple preparation.

ACIDIC INGREDIENTS Fresh lemon or lime juice and vinegars of all types add a touch of sharpness to a dish. Sometimes a few drops are all that's needed to heighten the flavors. Often when you think more salt is needed, a little acid will show you that it's not. Citrus juice and vinegars also contribute their own distinctive flavors— the brightness of lemon, the depth of an oak-aged red wine vinegar—to a dish.

FRESH HERBS Fresh herbs have a floral complexity that disappears when they are dried, so fresh herbs are generally best. Herbs are usually added both at the beginning of cooking, to contribute an underpinning of flavor, and then again just before serving, when their fragrance will blossom.

Serving Vegetables

The recipes in this book are designed as side dishes of four to six servings. But some of them, such as the gratins or

stuffed tomatoes, can also be served as main courses. Or, a vegetable dish can be offered as a first course, followed by a simple rice timbale, polenta, or pasta. Many of the serving ideas that accompany the master recipes expand on some of these suggestions.

Some vegetable dishes are good served warm, but most taste best when piping hot. To keep them that way, you need to warm your serving dishes. (This is especially true at high altitudes where food cools quickly.) Put serving dishes in your oven set to 200°F (95°C) to warm while you cook your vegetables. They will be ready in about 15 minutes.

Garnishing Vegetable Dishes

Vegetables, like many other foods, often benefit from the addition of a well-chosen garnish. Minced herbs that echo those already used in the recipe work well. Bright yellow lemon wedges are a colorful choice, especially if they're meant to be used. Sprigs of fresh parsley are pretty, as is a chiffonade (fine shreds) of arugula (rocket) or basil or finely slivered red or yellow bell pepper. And a drizzle of olive oil adds not only flavor but also an attractive glossy sheen.

1

Basic Recipes

In this chapter, you will find straightforward recipes that teach you how to cook a variety of vegetables using four common techniques: steaming, braising, sautéing, and roasting. After practicing these everyday recipes, you will have the building blocks needed to create countless other vegetable dishes. Each of the recipe chapters that follow is based on one of these methods.

Basic Steamed Vegetables

Steaming vegetables is quicker than boiling them because you don't need to wait for a large amount of water to heat. It is also an ideal method for anyone on a restricted diet, as any fats or seasonings are added after the vegetable is done, either by the cook or at the table.

1½ lb (750 g) cauliflower, broccoli, Brussels sprouts, or other vegetable suitable for steaming

1 tablespoon unsalted butter or olive oil

¼ teaspoon sea salt

Pinch of freshly ground pepper

MAKES 4–6 SERVINGS

1 **Ready the equipment**
You will need a steaming apparatus, either a collapsible metal basket that stands on short legs in a saucepan, or a perforated insert that fits into the top of a pan. You also need a tight-fitting lid for the pan so that no steam escapes. Preheat the oven to 200°F (95°C) and place a serving bowl in the oven to warm.

2 **Trim the vegetables**
Rinse the vegetables well. Next, trim away any tough or blemished areas from the vegetables. For cauliflower, use a paring knife to trim away any leaves and cut out the dense inner core; turn to page 39 if you need help. For broccoli, trim and peel the stalks; see page 38 for more details. For Brussels sprouts, trim the stem ends, then discard any withered or yellowed leaves; refer to page 42 if needed.

3 **Cut the vegetables into pieces**
Next, cut the vegetables into bite-sized pieces. Pieces that are the same size will cook evenly and at the same rate. For cauliflower, cut the crown into florets and then cut the florets into large bite-sized pieces. For broccoli, cut off the stalks below the crowns, then cut the stalks and crowns into large bite-sized pieces. For Brussels sprouts, cut any larger sprouts into halves or quarters through the core.

4 **Bring the water to a boil**
Pour water into the saucepan to a depth of about 1 inch (2.5 cm). Place the steamer basket or steamer insert in the pan. The water should come just up to the bottom of the steamer. Pour off or add water as needed. Cover and heat over high heat until large, vigorous bubbles form on the surface. (If you are not sure if the water is boiling, use a fork to lift up the steamer and take a peek.)

5 Steam the vegetables

Arrange the vegetable pieces in the steamer basket or steamer insert, distributing them evenly. Spacing the pieces evenly allows the steam to circulate around them more easily. Cover the pan and let the vegetables steam until tender and bright (if steaming green vegetables), about 5 minutes for cauliflower, 4 minutes for broccoli, or 8 minutes for Brussels sprouts.

6 Test the vegetables for doneness

Uncover the pan and insert the tip of the paring knife into a piece of vegetable. If the knife easily slips in and out, but the piece still offers a little firmness, the vegetables are done. If not, re-cover the pan, let the vegetables steam for another 30–60 seconds, and test again. Do not overcook the vegetables or they will lose their color and become mushy and unappealing and lack the fresh flavor of cooked vegetables at their best.

7 Remove the vegetables from the steamer

Using an oven mitt, grip the handle of the steamer basket or steamer insert and lift it out of the pan. Carefully shake it to release any excess water, and pour the vegetables into the warmed serving bowl.

8 Toss the vegetables with the seasonings

Add the butter or olive oil to the vegetables. The butter will melt and form a rich, creamy sauce. The olive oil will add a lighter flavor. Add the salt and pepper and gently toss with a silicone spatula to coat the vegetables evenly.

9 Adjust the seasonings and serve

Taste the vegetables. To heighten the flavors, add a bit more salt. Or, add more butter, olive oil, or pepper to suit your taste. Toss in each addition a little at a time and taste again until you are happy with the flavor balance. Serve right away.

CHEF'S TIP

If you plan to dress steamed vegetables later, cool them down quickly as soon as they've finished steaming to keep them from getting mushy. Hold them under running cold water until cool, shake off the excess water, and let drain before covering and refrigerating in a colander set on a plate.

RECOMMENDED USES

To dress up plain steamed vegetables, sprinkle with fresh lemon juice or chopped fresh herbs, or toss with Curry Butter (page 56) or Spicy Red Butter (page 119).

1¾–2 lb (875 g–1 kg) leeks, celery, fennel, or other vegetable suitable for braising

2 tablespoons unsalted butter

¼ cup (1½ oz/45 g) finely diced yellow onion (page 30)

¼ cup (2 fl oz/60 ml) dry white wine

1½ cups (12 fl oz/375 ml) chicken stock or canned low-sodium chicken broth

¼ teaspoon sea salt

⅛ teaspoon freshly ground pepper

1–2 teaspoons fresh lemon juice (page 38), optional

MAKES 4–6 SERVINGS

Basic Braised Vegetables

Braising, a gentle cooking method that calls for a small amount of liquid, low heat, and a covered pot, can be used for a variety of vegetables. A delicious advantage is that the cooking liquid, enhanced by the flavor of the vegetables as they braise, can be reduced and served as a companion sauce.

1 Ready the equipment

You will need a wide, shallow nonreactive pan with a tight-fitting lid (such as a lidded stainless-steel sauté pan), a wooden spoon, and tongs. Preheat the oven to 200°F (95°C) and place a serving platter or bowl in the oven to warm.

2 Prepare the vegetables

Rinse the vegetables well. Next, trim away any tough or blemished areas from the vegetables and then cut the vegetables into pieces. For leeks, cut off the tough green tops, leaving the white part with about 1 inch (2.5 cm) of the pale green leaves. Carefully trim away the roots, keeping the bases intact, and then cut the leeks in half lengthwise through the root end. Rinse the leeks well under running cold water, gently opening the leaves to flush out any sand. For celery, cut off the root end to separate the stalks, and rinse well. Trim away the top from each stalk at the joint along with any leaves. Using a vegetable peeler, remove the tough outer layer of strings from the stalks, running it the length of the curved edges. Cut the stalks crosswise into 4-inch (10-cm) lengths. For fennel, trim off the stems and feathery tops, or *fronds*, from the bulbs. Run a vegetable peeler over the bulbs to remove any bruised or tough portions. Cut each bulb in half through the core, then cut each of the halves into wedges; turn to page 41 if you need help. Be sure the vegetable pieces are uniform so that they will cook evenly.

3 Cook the onions and wine

Place the sauté pan over medium-high heat and add 1 tablespoon of the butter. When the butter has melted and the foam begins to subside, add the onion and cook, stirring frequently, until softened, 2–3 minutes. Add the wine and cook until the wine has cooked down, or *reduced*, by about one-half, 1–2 minutes.

4 Braise the vegetables

Add the vegetable pieces to the pan along with the chicken stock and salt. Raise the heat to high and bring to a boil. As soon as you see large bubbles begin to form, reduce the heat until only small bubbles occasionally break the surface. Cover the pan and let the vegetables braise in the enclosed cooking environment until tender, about 25 minutes for leeks, 15 minutes for celery, or 20 minutes for fennel.

5 Test the vegetables for doneness

Uncover the pan and insert the tip of a paring knife into a piece of vegetable. If the knife easily slips in and out, but the piece still offers a little firmness, the vegetables are done. If not, re-cover the pan, let the vegetables braise for another 2 minutes, and test again. Do not overcook the vegetables or they will become mushy and unappealing and lack the fresh flavor of cooked vegetables at their best. Using tongs, transfer the vegetables to the warmed serving platter, shaking off any excess liquid into the pan, and cover lightly with aluminum foil to keep warm.

6 Reduce the braising liquid to make a sauce

Return the pan with the braising liquid to high heat and bring to a boil. Let the liquid bubble vigorously until it is reduced to about ⅓ cup (3 fl oz/80 ml), about 8 minutes. Stir in the remaining 1 tablespoon butter and the pepper.

7 Adjust the seasonings and serve

Taste the sauce. It should taste like the vegetables that were cooked in it, with an underlying richness from the stock and the butter. If it tastes bland, add the lemon juice or more salt and pepper a little at a time until you are happy with the flavor balance. Pour the sauce over the vegetables and serve right away.

CHEF'S TIP

Vegetables will be dirtier or cleaner depending on where you got them. Most supermarket purchases have had some initial cleaning, but vegetables grown at home or those from a farmers' market may need more careful rinsing. If you find vegetables such as leeks or asparagus to be very dirty, soak them in a bowl of cool water for about 5 minutes to loosen any remaining soil.

RECOMMENDED USES

To dress up plain braised vegetables, sprinkle them with freshly grated Parmigiano-Reggiano cheese.

1½ lb (750 g) zucchini (courgettes) or other summer squash, bell peppers (capsicums), thick asparagus, or other vegetable suitable for sautéing

2 tablespoons olive oil

¼ teaspoon sea salt

Pinch of freshly ground pepper

MAKES 4–6 SERVINGS

Basic Sautéed Vegetables

Sautéing involves quickly cooking relatively tender vegetables in a small amount of fat over high heat. This sears the exterior, caramelizing it and creating a golden brown crust. Have your *mise en place* ready, and plan ahead so you sauté the vegetables at the last minute and serve them right away.

1 Ready the equipment

You will need a large frying pan (its sloping sides facilitate tossing the vegetables in the pan) and a wooden spoon or silicone spatula. Preheat the oven to 200°F (95°C) and place a serving dish in the oven to warm.

2 Trim the vegetables

Rinse the vegetables and pat them dry (excess water will cause them to splatter and steam rather than sear in the pan). Next, trim away any tough or blemished areas from the vegetables. For zucchini, trim the stem and blossom ends and discard. For bell peppers, cut off the stem ends and pull out the stems and clusters of seeds. Cut each pepper in half lengthwise to expose the white ribs. Brush away any lingering seeds, then use a paring knife to cut the ribs away. For thick asparagus, cut away the bottom of each spear where it starts to change color, becoming paler and visibly tougher. Using a vegetable peeler, peel the outer green skin from each spear to within about 2 inches (5 cm) of the tip.

3 Cut the vegetables into pieces

Next, cut the vegetables into bite-sized pieces. Pieces that are the same size will cook evenly and at the same rate. Zucchini is good quartered lengthwise, then cut crosswise into ½-inch (12-mm) pieces. The pepper halves are best cut lengthwise into slices about ⅜ inch (1 cm) thick. Asparagus are nice cut on the diagonal into larger 1½-inch (4-cm) pieces or smaller ¼-inch (6-mm) pieces.

4 Heat the pan

Place the pan over high heat and let it heat for a few moments. While the pan is heating, place all your ingredients near the stove. Hold your hand over the pan and when you feel the heat rising, add the olive oil.

5 Sauté the vegetables

As soon as the surface of the oil appears to shimmer, quickly add the vegetable pieces to the pan. Toss to coat with the oil and sprinkle with the salt and pepper. Move the vegetable pieces around in the pan briskly, either sliding the pan back and forth with little jerks to make them hop, or simply stirring with the wooden spoon or silicone spatula. (The first method reflects the origin of the word *sauté*, which comes from the French *sauter*, "to jump.")

6 Move the vegetables occasionally and test for doneness

Continue to sauté the vegetables, tossing or stirring them every 30 seconds or so at first, and then occasionally thereafter, until their color is vibrant and the pieces are golden in places and are tender but still slightly firm when pierced with the tip of a paring knife. This will take 8–10 minutes for zucchini or 4–7 minutes for bell peppers or asparagus. If the vegetables are not quite ready, sauté them for another 30–60 seconds, and test again. Remember not to stir the vegetables constantly; letting them have some contact with the hot pan will sear them and give them the special flavor that comes from high-heat cooking.

7 Remove the vegetables from the heat

As soon as the vegetables are ready, remove them from the heat to prevent them from overcooking. Let them cool in the pan for about 5 minutes to allow their flavors to develop.

8 Adjust the seasonings and serve

Taste the vegetables. To heighten the flavors, add a bit more salt. For a spicier flavor, add more pepper. Toss in each addition a little at a time and taste again until you are happy with the flavor balance. Pour the vegetables into the warmed serving dish and serve right away.

CHEF'S TIP

If you want to practice the classic sauté method—moving the food back and forth in the pan by means of quick, short jerking motions—fill a dry, unheated frying pan with dried beans. With repetition you'll soon develop the skill and confidence to try this with vegetables on a hot burner. And if you spill a few beans on the floor, you can simply pick them up and try again.

RECOMMENDED USES

To dress up plain sautéed vegetables, mix in a pinch of red pepper flakes, a bit of grated lemon or orange zest, or a splash of sherry or balsamic vinegar.

Basic Roasted Vegetables

Roasting in the dry heat of an oven is especially well suited to the dense vegetables that store well in the autumn and winter. Coated with a little olive oil and exposed to high heat, the natural sugars in the vegetables emerge. All that's needed to flavor them is some sea salt, pepper, and a savory fresh herb.

2 lb (1 kg) sweet potatoes; medium- or low-starch potatoes, such as Yukon gold or red potatoes; large carrots; or other vegetable suitable for roasting

¼ cup (2 fl oz/60 ml) olive oil

2 teaspoons chopped fresh thyme or rosemary (page 35)

½ teaspoon sea salt

⅛ teaspoon freshly ground pepper

MAKES 6 SERVINGS

1 Ready the equipment
You will need a heavy-duty roasting pan, a shallow baking dish, or a rimmed baking sheet large enough to hold the vegetables in a single layer. You will also need a large bowl and tongs or a wooden spatula. Position a rack in the middle of the oven and preheat the oven to 425°F (220°C). Place a serving dish on the stove top to warm from the heat of the oven.

2 Prepare the vegetables
Using a vegetable brush, scrub the vegetables well under running cold water and pat them dry. Next, peel the vegetables if needed and cut them into pieces. For long sweet potatoes, use a vegetable peeler to peel away the skins. Switch to a chef's knife and cut the sweet potatoes in half lengthwise. Cut each half into wedges. For regular potatoes, leave the skins on (they are nutritious and add flavor) and cut into wedges or 2½-inch (6-cm) chunks. For carrots, use a vegetable peeler to remove the skins. Switch to a chef's knife and trim off the leafy tops or stem ends and the rootlike tips. Cut the carrots into pieces about 2½ inches (6 cm) long. Cut the thickest chunks lengthwise into quarters and cut the medium chunks in half lengthwise. Always keep the vegetable pieces uniform so that they will cook evenly.

3 Toss the vegetables with the oil and seasonings
Put the vegetable pieces into the large bowl and add the olive oil, thyme, salt, and pepper. (If you are using regular potatoes, you'll want to do this quickly, as exposure to air will cause them to discolor. The oil will prevent discoloration.) Using your hands, toss the vegetables to coat them thoroughly.

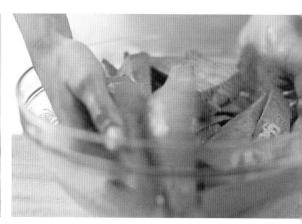

4 Roast the vegetables

Transfer the vegetables to the roasting pan with any remaining oil, and arrange them in a single layer without crowding. (Place the potato wedges with their cut sides up.) Doing so will expose the maximum surface area of the vegetables to the high heat of the oven and encourage even browning. Place the pan in the oven and let the vegetables roast until they are well browned and tender, about 20 minutes for sweet potatoes or 25 minutes for regular potatoes or carrots. Wearing long oven mitts and using a wooden spatula or tongs, turn or stir the vegetables about halfway through the roasting time to help them cook evenly.

5 Test the vegetables for doneness

Insert the tip of a paring knife into a vegetable piece. If the knife easily slips in and out, the vegetables are done. If not, let the vegetables roast for another 5 minutes and test again. Do not overcook the vegetables or they will become soft and unappealing and lack the flavor and texture of roasted vegetables at their best.

6 Adjust the seasonings and serve

Taste the vegetables. They should carry their own natural flavors and have a subtle sweetness that comes from roasting at a high heat, as well as accents of salt, pepper, and thyme. If you feel they taste bland, sprinkle salt over the pieces a little at a time to heighten the flavors. Transfer the vegetables to the warmed serving dish and serve right away.

CHEF'S TIP

For easy cleanup when roasting, line the pan or dish with aluminum foil before adding the vegetables. Place the shiny side of the foil outward, which deflects the heat most effectively, promoting even cooking.

RECOMMENDED USES

To dress up plain roasted vegetables, sprinkle them with fleur de sel, a coarse sea salt, or more chopped fresh herbs.

2

Key Techniques

The most time-consuming part of many vegetable recipes is getting the vegetables ready to cook. This chapter shows you step-by-step how to prepare a number of different vegetables and other essential items, from dicing a shallot to slicing fennel to stemming and rinsing spinach quickly and easily. Refer to this section whenever you need extra help preparing your ingredients.

Dicing an Onion

TECHNIQUE

1 Cut the onion in half

Using a chef's knife, cut the onion in half lengthwise, through the root end. This makes it easier to peel and gives each half a flat side for stability when you make your cuts.

2 Peel the onion

Using a paring knife, pick up the edge of the onion's papery skin at the stem end and pull it away. If the first layer of onion has rough or papery patches, remove it, too.

3 Place the onion on a board

Trim each end neatly, leaving some of the root intact to help hold the onion half together. Place an onion half, flat side down, on a cutting board with the root end facing away from you.

4 Cut the onion lengthwise

Hold the onion securely on either side. Using a chef's knife, make a series of lengthwise cuts as thick as you want the final dice to be. Do not cut all the way through the root end.

5 Cut the onion horizontally

Spread your fingers across the onion to help keep it together. Turn the knife blade parallel to the cutting board and make a series of horizontal cuts as thick as you want the final dice to be.

6 Cut the onion crosswise

Still holding the onion together with your fingers, cut it crosswise to make dice. Dicing an onion in this methodical way gives you pieces that cook evenly.

Dicing a Shallot

1 Separate the cloves

Sometimes you'll find plump, individual bronze-skinned shallots; other times they resemble garlic heads, with 2 or more cloves attached to one another. Separate the cloves.

2 Cut the shallot in half

When you are first learning to dice shallots, you may want to use a paring knife. As you gain skill, you can switch to a larger knife. Cut the shallot in half lengthwise, through the root end.

3 Peel and trim the shallot

Using the knife, pick up the edge of the shallot's papery skin and pull it away. Trim each end neatly, but leave some of the root intact to help hold the shallot half together.

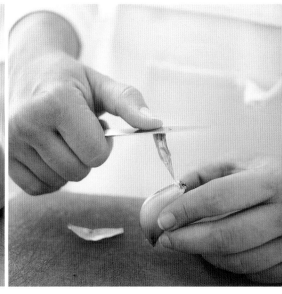

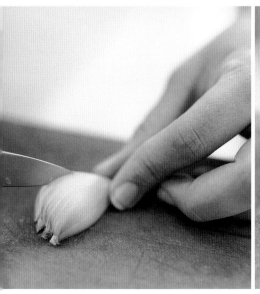

4 Cut the shallot lengthwise

Put the flat side of the shallot on the cutting board and make a series of thin lengthwise cuts. Do not cut all the way through the root end; it will hold the shallot layers together.

5 Cut the shallot horizontally

Turn the knife blade parallel to the cutting board and make a series of thin horizontal cuts.

6 Cut the shallot crosswise

Now, cut the shallot crosswise to make dice. Dicing a shallot in this methodical way gives you pieces that cook evenly.

Working with Garlic

1 Loosen the garlic peel
Using the flat side of a chef's knife, firmly press against the clove. If you plan to mince the garlic, it's fine to smash it. If you are slicing it, use light pressure to keep the clove intact.

2 Peel and halve the clove
The pressure from the knife will cause the garlic peel to split. Grasp the peel with your fingers and pull off and discard it. Using the chef's knife, cut the garlic clove in half lengthwise.

TROUBLESHOOTING
You may see a small green sprout running through the middle of a garlic clove. If left in, it could impart a bitter flavor to the recipe. Use the tip of a paring knife to pop out the sprout, and then discard it.

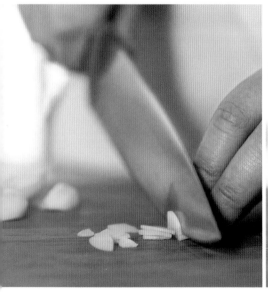

3 Cut the garlic into slices
One at a time, cut the garlic clove halves into very thin slices. Gather the slices in the center of the cutting board to cut into smaller pieces.

4 Chop the garlic
Hold the knife handle with one hand and rest the fingertips of your other hand on the knife tip. Rock the knife blade up and down and back and forth over the garlic until evenly chopped.

5 Mince the garlic
Gather the chopped garlic in a compact pile on the board. Clean the garlic bits off the knife and add them to the pile. Continue to chop until the garlic pieces are very fine, or *minced*.

Working with Green Onions

1 Trim the roots
Green (spring) onions are the young, immature shoots of the bulb onion. Using a chef's knife, trim off the roots.

2 Trim the tops
Remove any wilted or browned leaves. You want to use only the white and often the tender green portion of the onions, so trim off the tough green tops of the long, flat leaves.

TROUBLESHOOTING
When preparing green onions, be sure to feel the outer layer; if it's slimy, remove it as you would with other onion varieties. Refrigerate green onions in a perforated plastic bag to keep them fresh as long as possible.

3 Slice, chop, or mince the onions
For thinly sliced green onions, line up the trimmed root ends and cut the onions crosswise into slices. To chop or mince the onions, rock the blade of the knife over the slices.

Working with Jalapeño Chiles

1 Remove the seeds and ribs
Cut the chile lengthwise into quarters, then cut away the stem and the seeds and ribs (if desired) to lessen the heat.

2 Dice the chile finely
Cut the quarters into strips about ⅛ inch (3 mm) wide. Line up the strips and cut them crosswise at ⅛-inch intervals. Wear a latex glove to protect your hand from the chile's heat.

Working with Small Leafy Herbs

1 Select the herb
Small leafy herbs such as tarragon (top left), flat-leaf (Italian) parsley (right), and cilantro (fresh coriander; bottom) are delicate. Select bright, fragrant herbs for the best flavor.

2 Pluck the leaves from the stems
After rinsing the herbs and patting them dry, grasp the leaves between your thumb and index finger and pluck them from the stems. Discard the stems and any discolored leaves.

Snipping Chives

1 Gather the chives
Discard any wilted or yellowed chives. After rinsing the chives and patting them dry, gather a small amount of the blades into a little bundle that fits comfortably in your hand.

3 Chop the leaves
Gather the leaves on a cutting board. Rest the fingertips of one hand on the tip of a chef's knife and rock the blade up and down and back and forth briefly over the leaves to chop coarsely.

4 Finely chop or mince the leaves
Continue to regather the leaves and rock the blade over them until they are chopped into small, even pieces (finely chopped), or into pieces as fine as possible (minced).

2 Snip the chives
Using kitchen scissors, finely snip the chives into small pieces or snip them into slightly longer lengths as directed. (Alternatively, use a very sharp chef's knife to cut the chives into slices.)

Working with Small Branched Herbs

1 Select the herb
Small branched herbs such as thyme (right), marjoram (left), and oregano (top) are a bit hardier than other herbs. Avoid bundles with limp stems or branches.

2 Pluck the leaves from the stems
After rinsing the herbs and patting them dry, remove the petal-like leaves by gently running your thumb and index finger down the stems. Discard the stems and any discolored leaves.

Working with Rosemary

1 Removing the leaves
To remove the sturdy leaves of rosemary, carefully run your thumb and index finger down the stems.

3 Chop the leaves
Gather the leaves on a cutting board. Rest the fingertips of one hand on the tip of a chef's knife and rock the blade up and down and back and forth briefly over the leaves to chop coarsely.

4 Finely chop or mince the leaves
Continue to regather the leaves and rock the blade over them until they are chopped into small, even pieces (finely chopped), or into pieces as fine as possible (minced).

2 Finely chop or mince the leaves
Resting the fingertips of one hand on the tip of a chef's knife, rock the blade over the leaves. You'll want to finely chop or mince rosemary since it has a strong flavor and sharp leaves.

Working with Large Leafy Herbs

1 Select the herb

Herbs such as basil (top left), sage (top right), and mint (bottom) have large leaves that are sometimes slivered and sometimes chopped. Avoid bunches with wilted or discolored leaves.

2 Pull the leaves from the stems

After rinsing the herbs and patting them dry, pull off the large leaves one at a time. Discard the stems and any discolored leaves.

Toasting Nuts & Seeds

1 Toast the nuts or seeds

Place the nuts or seeds in a single layer in a dry frying pan over medium heat. Stir often to prevent burning.

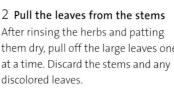

3 Stack and roll the leaves

Stack 5 or 6 leaves on top of one another, placing the smallest leaves on top. Roll the stack lengthwise into a tight cylinder. (Since sage leaves are narrow, you don't need to roll them.)

4 Cut the leaves into slivers

Using a chef's knife, cut the leaves crosswise into thin slivers. These slivers are known as a *chiffonade*. For chopped herbs, gather the slivers into a pile and rock the blade over them.

2 Let the nuts or seeds cool

When fragrant and/or golden, transfer the nuts or seeds to a plate to cool. Seeds will toast more quickly (usually about 3 minutes), while nuts may take longer (up to 5 minutes).

Making Fresh Bread Crumbs

1 Dry the bread, if necessary

Start with slices of slightly stale bread with a sturdy texture. Lay the bread slices flat on a sheet pan overnight to dry out, or use bread about 2 days past its peak of freshness.

2 Tear the slices into pieces

Fit a food processor with the metal blade. Then, tear the bread into small pieces and drop into the work bowl. Alternatively, drop the pieces into the container of a blender.

Dicing Bacon

1 Slice the bacon into strips

Stack 2 or 3 bacon slices on top of one another on the cutting board and cut them lengthwise into narrow strips. Use thick-cut bacon if possible for the most uniform dice.

3 Pulse to create crumbs

Pulse the food processor or blender until the bread pieces are chopped into small crumbs. You may need to do this in batches to ensure that the crumbs are processed evenly.

4 Pour the crumbs into a bowl

Pour the crumbs into a bowl to measure them for a recipe. You can use the crumbs plain or you can coat or brown the crumbs in butter or oil if directed.

2 Dice the bacon

Cut the bacon strips crosswise at ¼-inch (6-mm) intervals to create small dice.

Zesting & Juicing Citrus

1 Wash and grate the citrus

Wash the fruit well. Use a rasp grater, such as a Microplane grater, or the finest rasps on a box grater-shredder to remove the colored part of the peel, not the bitter white pith.

2 Clean off the grater

Don't forget to scrape all the zest from the back of the grater, where some of it naturally gathers.

Trimming Broccoli

1 Trim and peel the stalks

Using a paring knife, trim and discard any leaves and about 1 inch (2.5 cm) from the end of the stalk(s) if woody or tough. Using the knife or a vegetable peeler, peel the stalks.

3 Halve the citrus

First press and roll the citrus fruit firmly against the counter to break some of the membranes holding in the juice. Then, using a chef's knife, cut the fruit in half crosswise.

4 Juice the citrus

To extract as much juice as possible, use a citrus reamer to pierce the membranes as you squeeze. Catch the juice in a bowl. Strain it if necessary to remove the seeds before using.

2 Cut the crowns and stalks

Cut off each stalk just below the crown, then cut the crowns and stalks into large bite-sized pieces. (Or, leave the stalks attached and cut each "tree" lengthwise into halves or thirds.)

Trimming Cauliflower

TECHNIQUE

1 Cut out the core

Using a paring knife, trim and discard any leaves. Cut out the *core*, or dense portion in the base of the head, and remove it. If desired, peel the core, cut into pieces, and cook with the florets.

Working with Cabbage

TECHNIQUE

1 Halve the cabbage

Pull off any bruised or wilted outer leaves. Using a chef's knife, cut the cabbage in half through the dense inner core. For wedges, continue to cut each half lengthwise through the core.

2 Quarter the cabbage

If your recipe calls for thinly sliced cabbage, place the halves flat side down and cut them in half again to make quarters, again cutting lengthwise through the core.

2 Separate the florets

Separate the crown into florets by cutting through the stems. Cut any large florets into halves or quarters to create large bite-sized pieces. You can also peel and chop any stems.

3 Remove the core

Lay a quarter on the cutting board with a cut side facing down. Cut out the hard core. Repeat with the remaining quarters.

4 Cut into slices

Cut each cored cabbage quarter crosswise into thin slices as directed in the recipe, often about ¼ inch (6 mm) wide.

Stemming & Rinsing Greens

1 Sort through the leaves
Carefully sort through the leaves, examining each separately and discarding any leaves that are yellow (or otherwise discolored) or wilted or that have holes.

2 Tear the stems from tender greens
If working with tender greens such as spinach (shown here), fold each leaf in half along the stem with the vein side facing out. Grasp the stem with your other hand and quickly tear it away.

3 Cut the stems from tough greens
If working with tougher greens such as Swiss chard, kale, or collard greens (shown here), make a V-shaped cut on either side of the wide, thick stem to remove it from the leaf.

4 Rinse the leaves
Fill the bowl of a salad spinner with water. Insert the spinner basket, add the leaves, and swish to loosen any sand or grit. Lift the basket to change the water until no grit is visible.

5 Dry the leaves
Depending on the recipe, dry the leaves or let some of the rinsing water remain. For dry leaves, spin them in the salad spinner in batches until dry. For moist leaves, briefly drain them.

TROUBLESHOOTING
For bulky greens such as collards, stack a few leaves, roll up lengthwise, and cut crosswise into narrow ribbons before rinsing. Left whole, the leaves retain too much water, which runs all over the board during slicing.

Working with Fennel

1 Trim the stalks

Using a chef's knife, cut away the stalks and feathery leaves, or *fronds*, of the bulbs. Set aside some of the fronds if directed to use as a garnish or to add flavor.

2 Remove any bruised parts

Run a vegetable peeler over the outer layer of the bulbs to remove any bruised or tough portions. If the outer layer is badly bruised or scarred, remove it entirely.

3 Halve the fennel bulbs

Using the chef's knife, cut the fennel bulbs in half from top to bottom, cutting right through the core.

4 Cut the halves into wedges

If your recipe calls for wedges, cut each half lengthwise into about 4 wedges. Do not remove the core; it helps keep the layers together.

5 Cut the fennel into thin slices

If your recipe calls for thin slices, cut out the core if directed (leaving the core will keep the layers together). Then cut the halves into slices lengthwise or crosswise.

6 Mince the fronds (optional)

Rinse the fronds and dry well, then separate them from their stems. Using the chef's knife, rock the blade over the fronds until they are evenly chopped into fine pieces, or *minced*.

Preparing Brussels Sprouts

1 Trim the stem ends
Using a paring knife, trim the stem end of each Brussels sprout. Remove any withered or yellowed leaves.

Working with Round Vegetables

1 Trim the ends
Using a chef's knife, cut a slice off the top and bottom ends (a rutabaga is shown here). Stand the vegetable upright on a cutting board, using your fingers to hold it steady at the top.

2 Peel the skin
Using a paring knife and following the contour of the vegetable, slice away the peel in long strokes. With practice, you may be able to peel small items while holding them in your hand.

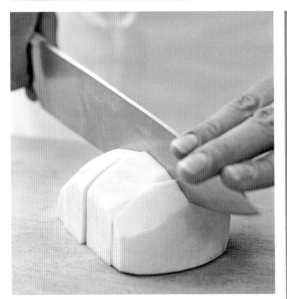

2 Cut the Brussels sprouts
Cut larger sprouts into halves or quarters through the core to make them about the same size as the smallest ones. This way, all the sprouts will cook in the same amount of time.

3 Cut the vegetable
Switch back to the chef's knife and cut the vegetable into pieces as directed. Many recipes will recommend cutting into 2-inch (5-cm) chunks or wedges.

TROUBLESHOOTING
When peeled and exposed to the air, some pale root vegetables discolor. If not using them right away, keep peeled potatoes in cool water. For rutabagas and celery root (celeriac), add a little lemon juice to the water.

Preparing Winter Squash

1 Halve the squash
Using a large chef's knife, cut the neck off the squash if directed. Cut both sections in half through the stem end.

Preparing Fresh Mushrooms

1 Brush away the dirt
Using a mushroom brush, gently brush away any dirt from the mushrooms. Use a damp cloth or paper towel to wipe away any stubborn dirt. (Button mushrooms may be briefly rinsed.)

2 Trim the stems
Using a paring knife, trim a thin slice from the base of the stem of each mushroom and discard. These pieces can be dry.

2 Scoop out the seeds
Using a metal spoon, scoop out and discard the seeds and any strings from each half as needed. (The neck sections of butternut squash don't contain seeds or strings.)

TROUBLESHOOTING

If the whole stem is tough, trim it away entirely. Some varieties, such as shiitake, always have tough, woody stems. Be sure to remove the stems on these mushrooms to avoid tough bits in your final dish.

3 Remove the gills, if necessary
If using portobellos, remove the dark gills, which will discolor other ingredients during cooking. Use a metal spoon to remove the gills, then cut the caps as directed.

Steamed & Boiled Vegetables

Almost any vegetable can be steamed or boiled, making these two techniques a good place to start. Both methods rely on boiling water, which surrounds the vegetables completely in a large pot or cooks them from below in the form of hot steam. The most important lesson to learn in these recipes is how to recognize when a vegetable is tender yet still bright and crisp.

Classic Mashed Potatoes

Russets are the classic mashing potato because their dry, highly starchy flesh readily absorbs butter and milk. Medium-starch varieties, such as Yukon gold, a favorite in part for its buttery color, also work well. Different mashing tools offer two distinct textures, one lumpy, the other smooth.

1 Prepare the potatoes

When using high-starch potatoes such as russet, consider leaving them whole and unpeeled (the skin adds flavor). Also, high-starch potatoes have dry, absorbent flesh, which means they readily take on cooking water if they are peeled and cut up. This prevents them from properly absorbing the milk and butter that are added later. Whether or not you plan to peel the potatoes, scrub and rinse them well. If using whole potatoes, put them in a 5-qt (5-l) pot or saucepan. (Alternatively, if you are using medium-starch potatoes or if you are short on time—whole potatoes take longer to cook—peel the potatoes and cut them into 2-inch/5-cm chunks. If you need help, turn to page 42. Have ready a 5-qt/5-l pot or saucepan half full of water. Transfer the chunks to the water to prevent discoloring.)

2 Cook the potatoes

If using whole potatoes, add water to the pot to cover the potatoes by 1 inch (2.5 cm). If using chunks, add more water to the pot if needed to cover them by 1 inch. Add 1 teaspoon of the salt to the water to season the potatoes. Place the pot over high heat and bring the water to a boil. As soon as you see large bubbles form, reduce the heat until only small bubbles occasionally break the surface. Cover the pot and simmer the potatoes until they are tender when pierced with the tip of a paring knife, 25–30 minutes for whole potatoes or about 18 minutes for chunks.

3 Peel the potatoes, if using whole potatoes

Using tongs, transfer the potatoes to a cutting board. Drain the water from the pot and set the pot aside. Using the tip of the paring knife, slit the skin of each potato lengthwise to create a starting place for peeling. Working with 1 potato at a time, and using a fork to hold it securely, peel off the skin with the tongs. Put the peeled potatoes in the reserved pot, cover, and set aside. Discard the skins.

4 Drain and dry the potatoes, if using chunks

Set a large colander in the sink. Using oven mitts and tilting the pot away from you to avoid the hot steam, pour the potatoes into the colander to drain. Return the drained potato chunks to the empty pot and place over low heat. Let the potatoes dry over the heat for about 1 minute, shaking the pot occasionally, to rid them of the extra moisture that can dilute flavor. Cover the pot and set aside.

5 Decide which mashing method you will use

Depending on the texture you desire, or the tools you have on hand, pick a mashing method. The handheld masher will yield a rougher texture; turn to page 49. The ricer method will result in smooth potatoes; turn to page 50.

2½ lb (1.25 kg) high-starch potatoes such as russet or medium-starch potatoes such as Yukon gold

1½ teaspoons sea salt

½ cup (4 fl oz/125 ml) milk or half-and-half (half cream)

6 tablespoons (3 oz/90 g) unsalted butter, at room temperature

⅛ teaspoon freshly ground white pepper

MAKES 4–6 SERVINGS

CHEF'S TIP
You can use a variety of liquids to make mashed potatoes, including skim, fat-reduced, or whole milk; half-and-half; and soy milk. The higher the butterfat, the richer the potatoes will be. You can also use the cooking water: just ladle out some of the water at the end of step 2 before draining the potatoes.

It's important to keep the liquid warm when making mashed potatoes. Cold milk will give the finished potatoes a heavy texture.

Soft room-temperature butter melts more quickly and evenly and will be easier to mix into the mashed potatoes.

Handheld Masher Method

1 **Warm the milk or half-and-half**
It is important to warm the liquid used for mashing potatoes because it keeps the potatoes warm and ensures that their final texture will be light. (Adding cold milk to hot potatoes causes the potato starch to seize, resulting in a gluey texture.) Pour the milk into a small saucepan and place over medium heat to warm. Watch closely and remove the liquid from the heat when you see small bubbles begin to form around the edges; you don't want it to burn. Meanwhile, preheat the oven to 200°F (95°C) and place a serving bowl in the oven to warm.

2 **Mash the potatoes**
Using a handheld masher breaks up the potatoes quickly and produces somewhat lumpy mashed potatoes, especially if you are using a medium-starch potato variety. Some people find this rougher texture appealing. Press down on the potatoes, turning the masher a little each time and working your way around the pot 1 or more times as needed to break up the potatoes well. Be sure you get the potatoes in the middle and at the edges of the pot, but don't feel you have to work them into a perfect texture at this point; you'll use a spoon to mix them next.

3 **Stir in the butter and warm milk**
Place the pot with the potatoes over low heat. Switch to a wooden spoon (using a spoon will yield smoother mashed potatoes) and mix the butter into the potatoes; room-temperature butter melts more readily into the potatoes than butter straight from the refrigerator. Next, pour in the warm milk, adding it in ¼-cup (2–fl oz/60-ml) increments. You may not need all of it. Stir in milk just until the potatoes are as light and smooth as you would like and seem as if they can't absorb any more liquid. Mix in the remaining ½ teaspoon salt and the white pepper.

4 **Adjust the seasonings and evaluate the consistency**
Taste the potatoes. If you feel they taste flat, stir in a little more salt and/or pepper, a pinch at a time. If you like creamier mashed potatoes, add a bit more warm milk or butter. Mix in each addition a little bit at a time and taste again until you are happy with the balance of flavors and the consistency. Stop mixing as soon as you reach the texture and flavors you like. Overmixing the potatoes will cause them to be gluey.

5 **Serve the potatoes**
Transfer the mashed potatoes to the warmed serving bowl, using a silicone spatula to scrape out any remaining potatoes from the pot. Serve right away.

Ricer Method

1 Warm the milk or half-and-half

It is important to warm the liquid used for mashing potatoes because it keeps the potatoes warm and ensures that their final texture will be light. (Adding cold milk to hot potatoes causes the potato starch to seize, resulting in a gluey texture.) Pour the milk into a small saucepan and place over medium heat to warm. Watch closely and remove the liquid from the heat when you see small bubbles begin to form around the edges; you don't want it to burn. Meanwhile, preheat the oven to 200°F (95°C) and place a serving bowl in the oven to warm.

2 "Rice" the potatoes

Using a ricer yields silky-smooth mashed potatoes. Transfer the potatoes to a large bowl and reserve the pot. If using a ricer with a choice of disks, fit it with one of the disks with large holes. You want to use the large holes because the potatoes will pass through them more easily. Using a large spoon, place some of the potatoes in the ricer. Close the handles and squeeze them together to pass the potatoes through the ricer, allowing them to fall back into the warm cooking pot; the warmth from the pot will help keep the potatoes light. Repeat to run all of the potatoes through the ricer into the pot.

3 Stir in the butter and warm milk

Place the pot with the potatoes over low heat. Switch to a wooden spoon and mix the butter into the potatoes; room-temperature butter melts more readily into the potatoes than butter straight from the refrigerator. Next, pour in the warm milk, adding it in ¼-cup (2–fl oz/60-ml) increments. You may not need all of it. Stir in milk just until the potatoes are light and seem as if they can't absorb any more liquid. Mix in the remaining ½ teaspoon salt and the white pepper.

4 Adjust the seasonings and evaluate the consistency

Taste the potatoes. If you feel they taste flat, stir in a little more salt and/or pepper, a pinch at a time. If you like creamier mashed potatoes, add a bit more warm milk or butter. Mix in each addition a little bit at a time and taste again until you are happy with the balance of flavors and the consistency. Stop mixing as soon as you reach the texture and flavors you like. Overmixing the potatoes will cause them to be gluey.

5 Serve the potatoes

Transfer the mashed potatoes to the warmed serving bowl, using a silicone spatula to scrape out any remaining potatoes from the pot. Serve right away.

Serving ideas

Few foods are more appealing than a simple mound of creamy mashed potatoes, but here are three ways you can vary your presentation. Use the potatoes as a bed for other foods such as grilled meats, rather than serving the potatoes alongside. Mash the potatoes with with their skins intact for added flavor and texture. Finally, if you have leftover mashed potatoes, use them to make old-fashioned mashed-potato pancakes.

A bed of mashed potatoes (top left)
Serve main dishes such as pork chops atop a bed of mashed potatoes. The juices from the meat and any gravy meld deliciously with the soft potatoes.

Smashed potatoes (left)
Cook unpeeled whole potatoes and "smash" them with a handheld masher. Be sure to use organic potatoes; the skins of commercially grown potatoes may contain pesticide residue.

Mashed-potato pancakes (above)
Leftover refrigerated mashed potatoes are firm enough to form into disks. In a nonstick frying pan over medium heat, warm 2 tablespoons olive oil and fry the disks until golden, 5 minutes per side.

Mashed Potato Variations

Now that you've learned how to turn simple boiled potatoes into a dish of light, fluffy Classic Mashed Potatoes (page 47) with the addition of milk and butter, you can vary these three ingredients to make countless other dishes, six of which are given here. The neutral potato can be paired with other vegetables, from celery root, turnip, and cabbage to green onions and garlic, and the fat can change from butter to olive oil. Tangy buttermilk along with some equally tangy fresh goat cheese can replace milk. Nearly every herb complements potatoes, too, and here a basil purée turns the humble white tubers a handsome pale green. Each variation makes 4 to 6 servings.

Mashed Potatoes with Olive Oil & Garlic

Garlic is a natural complement to mashed potatoes. Here, the garlic is first steeped in olive oil to soften its bite and infuse the oil.

In a small frying pan over low heat, warm ¼ cup (2 fl oz/60 ml) extra-virgin olive oil. Add 1 tablespoon minced garlic and cook, stirring often, until the oil is infused with garlic flavor but the garlic has not browned, about 10 minutes. Set aside.

In a small saucepan over low heat, warm 1 cup (8 fl oz/250 ml) milk until small bubbles form around the edges. Stir in the olive oil–garlic mixture and set aside while you cook the potatoes.

Cook 2½ lb (1.25 kg) potatoes, either whole or peeled and cut into chunks, in boiling salted water until tender. Peel the whole potatoes and return to the pot, or drain and dry the potato chunks.

Mash or rice the potatoes, then gradually stir in the warm milk mixture followed by ½ teaspoon sea salt and ⅛ teaspoon freshly ground white pepper. Taste and adjust the seasonings and consistency. Serve right away.

Mashed Potatoes with Basil Purée

These basil-scented mashed potatoes count on the high-starch russet to drink up the cooking water. This allows the clean herbal notes of the basil to come through with little or no additional liquid.

Peel 2½ lb (1.25 kg) russet potatoes and cut them into chunks. Cook the potato chunks in boiling salted water until tender, then drain and dry.

Meanwhile, make the basil purée: Bring a saucepan three-fourths full of water to a boil. Plunge 3 cups (3 oz/90 g) stemmed basil leaves in the boiling water and blanch until bright green, about 30 seconds. Rinse the leaves under running cold water and drain. Put the basil in a blender and add 1 teaspoon coarsely chopped garlic, ½ cup (4 fl oz/125 ml) extra-virgin olive oil, and ½ teaspoon sea salt. Process to a smooth purée, then add ½ cup (2 oz/60 g) freshly grated Parmigiano-Reggiano cheese and blend just until combined.

Mash or rice the potatoes, then stir in the basil purée. Taste and adjust the seasonings and consistency, gradually adding up to ½ cup (4 fl oz/125 ml) warm milk if needed. Serve right away.

Buttermilk Mashed Potatoes with Goat Cheese

Buttermilk and goat cheese give mashed potatoes a pleasant tangy flavor, which goes especially well with rich meats.

Cook 2½ lb (1.25 kg) potatoes, either whole or peeled and cut into chunks, in boiling salted water until tender. Peel the whole potatoes and return to the pot, or drain and dry the potato chunks.

Meanwhile, in a small saucepan over low heat, warm ¾ cup (6 fl oz/180 ml) buttermilk. Do not let the buttermilk boil, or it may separate.

Mash or rice the potatoes, then stir in 6 tablespoons (3 oz/90 g) room-temperature unsalted butter. Gradually add the warm buttermilk followed by ¼ lb (125 g) room-temperature fresh goat cheese, 2 teaspoons finely snipped fresh chives, ½ teaspoon sea salt, and ⅛ teaspoon freshly ground white pepper. Taste and adjust the seasonings and consistency. Serve right away, sprinkling more snipped chives over the top.

Mashed Potatoes with Cabbage & Green Onions

This recipe is a cross between two traditional Irish dishes, colcannon (mashed potatoes and pale green cabbage) and champ (mashed potatoes combined with green onions).

Cook 2½ lb (1.25 kg) potatoes, either whole or peeled and cut into chunks, in boiling salted water until tender. Peel the whole potatoes and return to the pot, or drain and dry the potato chunks.

Meanwhile, thinly slice and then chop ½ small head green cabbage (about 3 cups/9 oz/280 g). Put the cabbage in a frying pan over medium heat and add ¾ cup (6 fl oz/180 ml) milk, 6 tablespoons (3 oz/90 g) unsalted butter, ½ teaspoon sea salt, and ⅛ teaspoon freshly ground white pepper. Stir in 1 bunch chopped green (spring) onions (white and tender green parts; about 1 cup/3 oz/90 g), and cook, stirring occasionally, until the cabbage is tender, 12–15 minutes.

Transfer the cabbage mixture to the pot with the potatoes. Using a handheld masher, mash the vegetables until smooth. Most of the cabbage will disappear into the potatoes, leaving bits of green throughout. Stir in ½ teaspoon sea salt and ⅛ teaspoon freshly ground white pepper. Taste and adjust the seasonings and consistency. Serve right away.

Mashed Potatoes & Celery Root

The clean, celery-like flavor of celery root echoes the earthiness of the potatoes. Celery root mashes beautifully, and you can use more or less than the amounts indicated in this recipe. Because celery root is not starchy, the more you use, the lighter the finished dish will be.

Have ready a 1–1½ lb (500–750 g) celery root (celeriac) and enough potatoes to make a total of 2½ lb (1.25 kg) vegetables. Peel the celery root by cutting away the thick, gnarled skin with a sharp knife. Rinse under running cold water. Cut the celery root into 2-inch (5-cm) chunks and transfer to a 5-qt (5-l) pot or saucepan half full of cold water.

Peel and cut the potatoes into 2-inch (5-cm) chunks, adding them to the pot with the celery root. Cook the vegetables in boiling salted water until tender, then drain and dry.

Mash or rice the vegetables, then stir in 6 tablespoons (3 oz/90 g) room-temperature unsalted butter, ½ teaspoon sea salt, and ⅛ teaspoon freshly ground white pepper. Taste and adjust the seasonings. You probably won't need to add any additional liquid to this recipe since the celery root isn't starchy, but if the mixture seems too thick, gradually add up to ½ cup (4 fl oz/125 ml) warm milk. Serve right away.

Mashed Yukon Gold Potatoes & Turnips

Both the nutty-sweet flavor and yellow color of Yukon gold potatoes pair well with the bracing but sweet white-fleshed turnip. Fresh thyme adds an earthy note.

Peel and cut 1½ lb (750 g) Yukon gold potatoes into 2-inch (5-cm) chunks, adding them to a 5-qt (5-l) pot or saucepan half full of cold water. Peel 1 lb (500 g) turnips if necessary (large winter turnips require peeling, but tender summer ones do not). Cut the turnips into 1½-inch (4-cm) chunks, and add to the pot with the potatoes. Add 1 small sprig fresh thyme. Cook the vegetables in boiling salted water until tender, then drain and dry, discarding the thyme sprig.

In a small saucepan over medium heat, warm ½ cup (4 fl oz/125 ml) milk until small bubbles form around the edges.

Mash or rice the vegetables, then stir in 6 tablespoons (3 oz/90 g) room-temperature unsalted butter. Gradually stir in the warm milk followed by 1 teaspoon chopped fresh thyme, ½ teaspoon sea salt, and ⅛ teaspoon freshly ground white pepper. Taste and adjust the seasonings and consistency. Serve right away.

Steamed Broccoli with Lemon & Olive Oil

Broccoli steams to deep green tenderness in just minutes, whether cut into bite-sized pieces or into long spears with the stalks attached to the crowns. The heat of the broccoli renders the few simple seasonings—fruity olive oil, tangy lemon zest and juice, and mildly pungent green onions—bright and aromatic.

1½ lb (750 g) broccoli (about 3 large "trees")

¼ cup (2 fl oz/60 ml) extra-virgin olive oil

2 teaspoons finely grated lemon zest (page 38)

2 tablespoons fresh lemon juice (page 38)

2 tablespoons finely chopped green (spring) onion, white and tender green parts (page 33)

½ teaspoon sea salt

⅛ teaspoon freshly ground pepper

MAKES 4–6 SERVINGS

CHEF'S TIP
Some people discard the stalks of broccoli when steaming, but these parts are delicious, too. Thickly peel the stalks, removing about ⅛–¼ inch (3–6 mm) of the outer layer, then cut the stalks into large bite-sized pieces and cook along with the florets. When peeled and cut into pieces, the stems and core of cauliflower are also quite edible.

1 **Trim the broccoli**
If you are not sure how to trim broccoli, turn to page 38. With its clusters of florets crowning sturdy stalks, broccoli resembles trees. When you find them at the market, typical heads or bundles may be one large tree or several smaller ones. Using a paring knife, trim away and discard any leaves and about 1 inch (2.5 cm) from the end of each stalk. Using the knife or a vegetable peeler, peel each stalk and cut off just below the crown. Cut the crowns and stalks into large bite-sized pieces. (Alternatively, leave the peeled stalks attached and slice the larger trees into halves or in thirds.) Rinse under running cold water.

2 **Combine the seasonings**
In a bowl large enough to hold the broccoli comfortably, stir together the olive oil, lemon zest, lemon juice, green onion, salt, and pepper. Set aside.

3 **Steam the broccoli**
Preheat the oven to 200°F (95°C) and place a serving dish in the oven to warm. For more details on steaming vegetables, turn to page 20. Pour water into a saucepan to a depth of about 1 inch (2.5 cm). Set a collapsible steamer basket or steamer insert in the pan. The water should come just up to the bottom of the steamer. Pour off or add water as needed. Cover the pan and bring the water to a boil over high heat. Arrange the broccoli in the steamer basket, distributing it evenly. Cover the pan and steam the broccoli until it is bright green and tender, about 4 minutes. Test the stems for doneness with the tip of a paring knife—they should offer a little firmness but yield fairly easily. Cook for 1 minute longer if necessary. Do not overcook or the broccoli will become strong tasting and mushy.

4 **Toss the broccoli with the seasonings**
Using an oven mitt, grip the handle of the steamer basket and lift it out of the pan. Shake to remove any excess water and add the broccoli to the bowl with the olive oil mixture. Using a large silicone spatula, toss to coat evenly.

5 **Adjust the seasonings and serve**
Taste the broccoli. If you feel it needs more zip, add more salt, pepper, or lemon juice a little at a time until you are happy with the balance of flavors. You should be able to clearly taste the full, fresh flavor of the broccoli. Transfer the broccoli to the warmed serving dish and serve right away.

Steamed Vegetable Variations

In Steamed Broccoli with Lemon & Olive Oil (page 54), you discovered that a steamer basket or insert and a saucepan with a tight-fitting lid are all you need to steam a variety of vegetables. Greens such as bok choy will be done in minutes, while dense tubers, roots, and gourds, such as potatoes, beets, and winter squashes, will take longer. When steaming these dense vegetables, a steamer insert is a better choice than a basket because it allows you to use more water for longer cooking. Olive oil and butter are typical toppings, but here Asian sesame oil, flavored butters, and herb sauces are also used. Each variation makes 4 to 6 servings.

Cauliflower with Curry Butter

Here, creamy butter seasoned with bold spices complements cauliflower.

In a bowl, stir together **4 tablespoons (2 oz/60 g) room-temperature unsalted butter, 2 teaspoons curry powder, 1 teaspoon grated lemon zest, 1 teaspoon fresh lemon juice, ½ teaspoon sea salt, ¼ teaspoon sugar, ⅛ teaspoon ground mace, and ⅛ teaspoon hot paprika.** Set aside.

Cut out the core of a **1½–2 lb (750 g–1 kg) head cauliflower** and separate the crown into florets. Cut any large florets into large bite-sized pieces.

Set a steamer basket or steamer insert in a saucepan. Add water to come just up to the bottom of the steamer and bring to a boil. Arrange the cauliflower in the steamer. Cover the pan and steam until the cauliflower is tender yet firm, about 5 minutes.

Transfer the cauliflower to a warmed serving bowl. Add the curry butter and **2 tablespoons chopped fresh flat-leaf (Italian) parsley** and toss to coat evenly. Taste and adjust the seasonings. Serve right away.

New Potatoes with Butter, Shallot & Tarragon

Regardless of shape, color, or variety, freshly dug potatoes, with their delicate skins, are perfect for steaming.

Carefully scrub **1½–2 lb (750 g–1 kg) new potatoes** or other small potatoes. Set a steamer basket or steamer insert in a saucepan. Add water to come just up to the bottom of the steamer and bring to a boil. Arrange the potatoes in the steamer. Reduce the heat to medium-high, cover the pan, and steam until tender yet firm, 30–40 minutes, depending on the size of the potatoes. Check the pan every 10 minutes and add more hot water if needed.

Meanwhile, in a large bowl, stir together **3 tablespoons finely diced unsalted butter, 2 tablespoons finely diced shallot, 2 tablespoons minced fresh tarragon, 2 tablespoons minced fresh flat-leaf (Italian) parsley, ¾ teaspoon sea salt, and ⅛ teaspoon freshly ground pepper.**

Transfer the potatoes to the bowl with the butter and herbs and toss to coat evenly. Taste and adjust the seasonings. Serve right away.

Baby Bok Choy with Sesame Oil

Small, compact baby bok choy takes only minutes to steam and is delicious with a few drops of dark sesame oil and toasted black and white sesame seeds.

Slice **4 baby bok choy, about ⅓ lb (155 g) each,** in half lengthwise. Soak them in a bowl of cold water for 15 minutes to loosen any sand or dirt that may be lodged in the base of the leaves, then rinse well.

Set a steamer basket or steamer insert in a saucepan. Add water to come just up to the bottom of the steamer and bring to a boil. Arrange the bok choy cut side down in the steamer. Cover the pan and steam until the leaves are bright green and the stems are tender yet firm, about 4 minutes.

Transfer the bok choy to a warmed platter, arranging them cut side up. Drizzle **¼ teaspoon Asian sesame oil** over each half. Sprinkle **½ teaspoon sea salt** over all the halves followed by **2 teaspoons *each* toasted black sesame seeds and white sesame seeds.** Serve right away.

Beets with Salsa Verde

Bright, acidic flavors, such as those found in the salsa verde used here, pair well with earthy beets.

Cut all but 1 inch (2.5 cm) of the stems from **6 medium to large beets or 12 small ones**. Rinse the beets well. Set a steamer basket or steamer insert in a saucepan. Add water to come just up to the bottom of the steamer and bring to a boil. Arrange the beets in the steamer. Reduce the heat to medium-high, cover the pan, and steam until tender, 25–40 minutes, depending on the size of the beets. Check the pan every 10 minutes and add more hot water if needed.

Meanwhile, make the salsa verde. In a bowl, stir together **⅓ cup (3 fl oz/80 ml) extra-virgin olive oil, 1 finely diced small shallot, ¼ cup (⅓ oz/10 g) finely chopped fresh flat-leaf (Italian) parsley, 2 tablespoons chopped fresh tarragon, 1 tablespoon rinsed capers, 1 teaspoon grated lemon zest, 1 minced garlic clove, ¼ teaspoon sea salt, and ⅛ teaspoon freshly ground pepper.**

One at a time, rinse the steamed beets under running cold water and slip off their skins, using a paring knife if needed. Trim away the stem and root ends. Cut the beets into wedges.

Transfer the beets to a bowl. Just before serving, stir **2 teaspoons fresh lemon juice** into the salsa verde. Add 2 tablespoons of the salsa verde to the bowl with the beets and mix well (reserve the remainder for another use). Taste and adjust the seasonings. Serve hot or warm.

Winter Squash with Sage & Pecan Butter

Steaming is an excellent way to soften the flesh of winter squashes, making it easy to enjoy such varieties as Perfection, blue hubbard, kabocha, and butternut.

Using a large chef's knife, cut a **2½–3 lb (1.25–1.5 kg) winter squash** in half through the stem end. Scoop out and discard the seeds. Cut each half into 2 or 3 pieces to fit a steamer basket or steamer insert. Sprinkle each piece with **⅛ teaspoon sea salt**, rubbing it lightly into the flesh.

Set the steamer basket or steamer insert in a saucepan. Add water to come just up to the bottom of the steamer and bring to a boil. Arrange the squash pieces flesh side down in the steamer. Reduce the heat to medium-high, cover the pan, and steam until tender, 30–45 minutes, depending on the variety of squash and its size. Check the pan every 10 minutes and add more hot water if needed.

Meanwhile, in a small frying pan over medium heat, melt **3 tablespoons unsalted butter**. Remove from the heat and stir in **⅓ cup (1½ oz/45 g) finely chopped toasted pecans, 1 tablespoon *each* finely chopped fresh sage and flat-leaf (Italian) parsley, 1 minced garlic clove, ¼ teaspoon sea salt, and ⅛ teaspoon freshly ground pepper.**

Transfer the squash to a warmed platter, placing the pieces flesh side up. Spoon the butter mixture evenly over the squash and serve right away.

Cabbage with Caraway Seeds & Sour Cream

Steaming showcases how delectable—and quickly cooked—cabbage can be. Take advantage of the pretty, crinkly leafed savoy variety, if available. Mildly flavored, it has puffy pockets in the leaves that nicely trap the seasonings.

Remove any bruised or wilted outer leaves from **1 head green cabbage**, then cut it in half through the core. Cut each half lengthwise into wedges 1½–2½ inches (4–6 cm) thick at the widest part, also going through the core to keep the layers joined together.

Set a steamer basket in a wide saucepan (avoid using a steamer insert for this recipe—the basket is wider, providing more space for the wedges). Add water to come just up to the bottom of the steamer and bring to a boil. Arrange the cabbage wedges in the steamer basket. Reduce the heat to medium-high, cover the pan, and steam until tender yet firm, 7–10 minutes.

Meanwhile, in a bowl large enough to hold the cabbage comfortably, stir together **3 tablespoons finely diced unsalted butter, 3 tablespoons sour cream, 1 teaspoon caraway seeds, ¼ teaspoon sea salt, and ⅛ teaspoon freshly ground pepper.**

Transfer the cabbage to the bowl with the sour cream mixture. Using a large silicone spatula, gently turn the wedges until lightly coated. Serve right away.

Green Beans & Yellow Wax Beans with Pesto

Boiling fresh beans in a big open pot of salted water is a simple way to a colorful, summery side dish. When mixing different beans for maximum visual appeal, cooking them separately is the key to perfect doneness for each type. Pesto is a perfect foil for newly harvested beans, adding color and a satisfying, savory depth.

1 Prepare the beans

Use a paring knife to cut off the stems of the green beans or bend the stems sharply between your fingers to remove them (the latter is referred to as *snapping*). Nowadays, most green beans have no "strings." If you do find a wispy string attached to the stem end, pull it along the length of the bean to remove it. If the beans are young and tender, you can leave the tails on. If not, or if the tails feel sharp, remove them with a paring knife or your fingers. Leave the green beans whole, or cut them on the diagonal into halves or thirds. Set aside. Repeat to prepare the wax beans and set them aside separately from the green beans.

2 Make the pesto

Put the garlic cloves in a large mortar and mash them several times with a pestle. A small handful at a time, add the basil leaves to the mortar and pound and mash them with the pestle (be patient—this process takes some time). Gradually add the pine nuts, using the pestle to crush and mash them into the basil. Using a spatula, transfer the mixture to a bowl and stir in the cheese. Still stirring, pour in the olive oil in a thin, steady stream to make a moderately thick paste. Stir in the ¼ teaspoon salt and the pepper. Taste and adjust the seasonings.

3 Cook the beans

Have ready 2 clean kitchen towels and a bowl large enough to hold all the beans comfortably. Place a 5-qt (5-l) saucepan three-fourths full of water over high heat and add the 2 teaspoons salt. When the water starts boiling, add the green beans and cook, uncovered, for about 2 minutes. Begin testing for doneness after 1 minute (slender, young green beans or haricots verts cook very quickly): Using a flat skimmer, remove a bean and bite into it. The beans are done when they are tender but still offer a little resistance; the time can vary from 1–3 minutes or up to 6–7 minutes, depending on the kind of bean. Using the skimmer, scoop the beans out and turn them onto a kitchen towel to absorb excess moisture. Repeat to cook the wax beans in the same pan of boiling water in the same way (they usually take longer to cook, 5–7 minutes), then turn them out onto the second towel.

4 Toss the beans and pesto

Transfer all the beans to the bowl and add 3 tablespoons of the pesto; save the remaining pesto for another use. Using a silicone spatula, toss the beans with the pesto. Taste and adjust the seasonings, adding a bit more salt or pesto if you feel it's needed. Transfer to a serving dish and serve hot or warm.

¾ lb (375 g) green beans such as Blue Lake or haricots verts

¾ lb (375 g) yellow wax beans

For the pesto

2 cloves garlic

2 cups (2 oz/60 g) packed fresh basil leaves, rinsed and dried

¼ cup (1 oz/30 g) pine nuts, toasted (page 36)

2 oz (60 g) freshly grated *pecorino romano* or Parmigiano-Reggiano cheese, or a mixture

½ cup (4 fl oz/125 ml) extra-virgin olive oil

¼ teaspoon sea salt

⅛ teaspoon freshly ground pepper

2 teaspoons sea salt

MAKES 4–6 SERVINGS

CHEF'S TIP

When adding salt to the water for boiling quick-cooking vegetables, add it first, before the water comes to a boil, so you won't forget. (The salt will help flavor the vegetables.) For long-cooking recipes, add the salt after the water comes to a boil. If salted water boils too long, it develops a minerally taste.

Corn on the Cob with Chile-Lime Butter

Corn eaten at the height of summer will be flavorful and tender if cooked as soon as possible after picking. Here, corn's natural sweetness is nicely balanced by a compound butter that carries the heat of chile, the tartness of lime, the duskiness of cumin, and the pungency of cilantro.

6–12 ears corn

For the chile-lime butter

4 oz (125 g) unsalted butter, at room temperature

⅓ cup (½ oz/15 g) finely chopped fresh cilantro (fresh coriander) (page 34)

2 green (spring) onions, white and tender green parts, minced (page 33)

1 jalapeño chile, seeded and finely diced (page 33)

Grated zest of 1 lime (page 38)

Juice of 1 lime (page 38)

½ teaspoon ground cumin

¼ teaspoon sea salt

MAKES 4–6 SERVINGS

CHEF'S TIP

Grilling corn gives it a toasty, slightly caramelized flavor. Prepare a hot fire for direct-heat grilling in a charcoal grill, or preheat a gas grill to high. Remove the husks and silks from the corn and brush the ears lightly with melted unsalted butter. Grill directly over the fire, turning the ears every 30 seconds or so, until the kernels are browned in places on all sides, about 5 minutes.

1 **Bring the water to a boil**
Bring a large pot three-fourths full of water to a boil over high heat. The pot needs to be big enough to accommodate the corn comfortably, but since the corn takes little time to cook, it can be boiled in 2 batches. (Alternatively, you can steam the corn in 2 batches, which is quicker because you heat a smaller amount of water. Pour water into a wide saucepan to a depth of about 1 inch/2.5 cm. Set a collapsible steamer basket in the pan—avoid using a steamer insert for this recipe since the basket is wider and provides more space for the corn. Add water to come just up to the bottom of the steamer and bring to a boil.)

2 **Shuck the corn**
While the water is heating, pull the husks off the ears of corn and discard them, then pull off the silks. Rub off any clinging silk with your hands or a damp kitchen towel. If the tips of the ears are dry or lacking kernels, use a chef's knife to cut them off. Leave the stalks intact as a handle, or cut them off as well.

3 **Cook the corn**
As soon as large bubbles begin breaking on the surface, add the ears and cook just until tender, 3–4 minutes. (Alternatively, if steaming the corn, arrange the ears in the steamer basket when the water comes to a boil. Cover the pan and steam just until the corn is tender, about 5 minutes.) To test for doneness, cut a slice off the end of an ear and take a bite. Place a clean kitchen towel on a platter to absorb the excess moisture, then use tongs to transfer the ears to the towel.

4 **Make the chile-lime butter**
While the corn is cooking, make the chile-lime butter: In a small bowl, combine the butter, cilantro, green onions, jalapeño, lime zest, lime juice, cumin, and salt. Mix well with a wooden spoon. Taste and evaluate the seasonings. If needed, add more salt or lime juice a little at a time to bring out the flavors.

5 **Serve the corn**
Transfer the corn to individual plates; if you removed the stalks, pin on decorative corn holders, if you like. Place an attractive dollop of the chile butter on each plate, or transfer the butter to a small serving bowl and pass at the table with a knife for spreading. Serve right away.

Braised Vegetables

Braising, like steaming and boiling, is a moist-heat method, but it cooks vegetables more gently in a smaller amount of liquid (often stock or wine) than boiling. To soften sturdy vegetables such as artichokes, you'll need to braise them for up to 20 minutes, but braising is also ideal for such tender vegetables as peas, which cook in just 3 to 4 minutes. In most cases, the braising liquid becomes a flavorful sauce.

Braised Artichokes with Shallots & Peas

This braise celebrates the spring appearance of artichokes and English peas, simmering them to tenderness with an aromatic mix of shallots, parsley, and lemon. A dollop of crème fraîche is used here to add a subtle tang and silkiness to the sauce and to tie all the elements of the braise together.

1 Zest and juice the lemons

To find out more about zesting and juicing citrus, turn to page 38. First, zest 1 of the lemons: Using a fine rasp grater, remove the colored part of the peel, taking care not to grate the bitter white pith underneath. Measure out 1 teaspoon zest and set it aside (you'll only need to zest 1 of the lemons for this recipe). Then, juice the same lemon: cut the lemon in half crosswise and, using a handheld reamer or a citrus juicer, squeeze out the juice. Repeat to juice the second lemon. Reserve the juiced lemon halves and set the juice and zest aside separately.

2 Remove the outer leaves and trim the artichokes

Fill a large glass or stainless-steel bowl half full of cold water and add the lemon juice. Adding the artichokes to this lemon water after you've trimmed them prevents them from turning brown. Working with 1 artichoke at a time, snap off the outer leaves until you reach the pale green leaves near the center. Using a serrated knife, cut off the top one-third of the artichoke to remove the pointed leaf tips. Rub the cut surface with a reserved juiced lemon half. As you work, continue using the lemon halves to rub the cut surfaces as you make them; this will also help to prevent browning.

3 Peel the stem and remove the choke

Using a paring knife, peel the stem and trim off the tiny, dark green leaves where the stem meets the base. Also, trim off the bottoms of the larger outer leaves where they snapped off. Using the serrated knife, cut the artichoke lengthwise into quarters. Switch back to the paring knife and remove and discard the fuzzy choke and any thorny inner leaves, which can be tough in large artichokes. Cut the quarters lengthwise into halves or thirds to create wedges. Transfer the wedges to the bowl of lemon water. Repeat to prepare the remaining artichokes, adding more water to the bowl just to cover the artichokes if needed. Don't worry if they discolor in spots—they'll even out when they are cooked.

4 Dice the shallots

If you are not sure how to dice a shallot, turn to page 31. Using a paring knife, cut the shallots in half lengthwise and peel each half. One at a time, place the shallot halves, cut side down, on the cutting board. Make a series of parallel vertical cuts, being sure to stop just short of the root end (this holds the shallot half together as you cut). Then make a series of parallel horizontal cuts and finally crosswise cuts to create ¼-inch (6-mm) dice. ❯

2 lemons

6 medium or large artichokes, about ½ lb (250 g) each

2 large shallots

3 tablespoons olive oil

1 sprig fresh thyme or ¼ teaspoon dried thyme

½ cup (4 fl oz/125 ml) dry white wine

1½ cups (12 fl oz/375 ml) chicken stock or canned low-sodium chicken broth, plus extra if needed for making the sauce

½ teaspoon sea salt

1 lb (500 g) fresh English peas in their pods or 1 cup (5 oz/155 g) frozen petite peas

1 small clove garlic

1 bunch fresh flat-leaf (Italian) parsley

6–8 leaves fresh mint

½ cup (4 oz/125 g) crème fraîche

1 teaspoon Dijon mustard

⅛ teaspoon freshly ground pepper

MAKES 4–6 SERVINGS

5

6
⌄

A mixture of dry white wine and chicken stock creates a flavorful braising liquid that is used later as the base for a creamy sauce to serve with the vegetables.

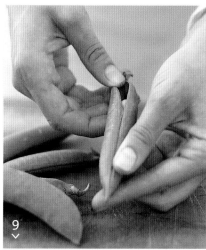

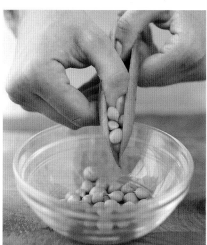

5 Cook the shallots

Select a wide, shallow nonreactive pan with a tight-fitting lid—a lidded sauté pan about 10 inches (25 cm) wide and 3 inches (7.5 cm) deep is a good choice. You can also use a braiser (a wide shallow pan with two handles and a domed lid) if you have one. Place the pan over medium-high heat and add the olive oil. When the surface of the oil appears to shimmer, it is sufficiently hot. Add the shallots and the thyme sprig. Stir with a wooden spoon to coat the shallots evenly with the oil and cook, stirring often, until fragrant, about 1 minute.

6 Lightly brown the artichokes

Working quickly, drain the artichokes in a colander and shake the colander to remove the excess water. Add the artichokes to the pan with the shallots, raise the heat to high, and cook, stirring occasionally, until the artichokes are lightly browned in places, about 5 minutes.

7 Reduce the wine

Add the wine and cook until the wine has thickened to a glazelike consistency and has cooked down, or *reduced,* to about 2 tablespoons, about 3 minutes.

8 Braise the artichokes

Preheat the oven to 200°F (95°C) and place a serving dish in the oven to warm. Add the chicken stock and salt to the pan and bring to a boil. As soon as you see large bubbles begin to form, reduce the heat to medium or medium-low until only small bubbles occasionally break the surface of the liquid. Cover the pan and simmer until the artichokes are tender when pierced with the tip of a paring knife, 12–15 minutes. Meanwhile, prepare the remaining ingredients.

9 Shell the peas

Removing the peas from their pods, or *shelling* them, just before cooking prevents them from drying out. Have ready a small bowl. Working with 1 pod at a time, pinch the tip at each end to begin splitting the pod. Squeeze the pod, pressing your thumb against the seam to continue opening it. Sweep your thumb down along the inside of the pod to pop out the peas from the pod and let them fall into the bowl. Discard the pod. Repeat to shell the remaining peas. You should have about 1 cup (5 oz/155 g) shelled peas.

10 Chop the garlic

For more details on working with garlic, turn to page 32. Place the clove on a cutting board, firmly press against it with the flat side of a chef's knife, and pull away the papery skin. Cut the clove in half lengthwise, then thinly slice the halves lengthwise. Gather the slices in a small pile on the board. With the fingertips of one hand resting on top of the tip of the knife, rock the blade up and down and back and forth over the garlic slices until evenly chopped. ›

11 Chop the parsley
To find out more about chopping small leafy herbs, turn to page 34. Pluck the leaves from the parsley sprigs and discard the stems. Gather the leaves in a small pile on the cutting board. Using the chef's knife, rock the blade over the leaves until they are coarsely chopped. Measure out 3 tablespoons of the chopped parsley.

12 Sliver the mint
If you need help slivering large leafy herbs, turn to page 36. Working in 2 batches, stack the mint leaves on top of one another. Roll the stack of leaves lengthwise as tightly as possible into a cylinder. Using the chef's knife, cut the leaves crosswise, which will create thin slivers. These slivers are known as a *chiffonade*. Measure out 1 tablespoon of the slivered mint.

13 Combine the garlic, herbs, and lemon zest
In a small bowl, combine the garlic, parsley, mint, and lemon zest. Stir with a fork to mix well and set aside.

14 Add the peas and make the sauce
When the artichokes are done, there should be at least ½ cup (4 fl oz/125 ml) of flavorful liquid left in the pan with them so you can make a sauce. If too much liquid has boiled away, add a little more stock or water as needed. It's fine to leave the whole thyme sprig in the finished dish (it adds a rustic touch), but you can remove it at this point if you like. Add the peas to the pan, then stir in the crème fraîche and mustard. Cook, stirring, still over medium or medium-low heat, until the crème fraîche melts into the pan juices to create a creamy, uniform sauce and the peas are heated through, about 2 minutes.

15 Adjust the seasonings and serve
Gently stir the herb mixture and the pepper into the vegetables. Taste the sauce and adjust the seasonings. To heighten the flavors, add a bit more salt. If it lacks zip, stir in more mustard or fresh mint. For a creamier sauce, stir in more crème fraîche, or for a thinner one, add more stock. Add each ingredient a little at a time until you are happy with the flavor balance and consistency. Transfer the artichokes and peas to the warmed serving dish and serve right away.

Serving ideas

Braised vegetables may be served not only as a simple side dish, but also as a topping for other preparations. The nutty flavor of artichokes mixed with sweet peas is a delicious combination with soft polenta or with pasta—neither overpowers the delicate flavors of the vegetables, and both benefit from the creamy sauce. Spooning this savory braise over a plain omelet is yet another way to showcase these spring flavors.

Over soft polenta (top left)
Thick, soft polenta makes an ideal base for the artichokes and peas, adding its own subtly sweet corn flavor. Use a vegetable peeler to create Parmigiano-Reggiano shavings as a garnish.

With pasta (left)
Use the braised vegetables to sauce pasta. Curly strands such as fusilli lunghi (shown here) wrap around the artichoke wedges, and the creamy braising liquid clings to the noodles.

With an omelet (above)
Spoon the braised artichokes and peas over a plain omelet, and you have a wholesome dish well suited for a simple dinner or hearty lunch.

Braised Fennel with White Wine & Tomato

Dense and sturdy fennel is perfect for braising, as it turns tender without losing its shape or pleasant firmness to the bite. Fennel seeds underscore the bulb's anise flavor, which is sharp and clean when raw but deep and subdued when cooked. The grated tomato cooks into a sauce, providing welcome acidity for this mellow vegetable.

6 small or 3 or 4 medium fennel bulbs, about 1¾ lb (875 g) total weight

4 or 5 small plum (Roma) tomatoes, about ½ lb (250 g) total weight

2 cloves garlic

¼ cup (2 fl oz/60 ml) extra-virgin olive oil

½ cup (4 fl oz/125 ml) dry white wine

½ teaspoon fennel seeds

1 cup (8 fl oz/250 ml) chicken stock, canned low-sodium chicken broth, or water

1 teaspoon sea salt

1 oz (30 g) Parmigiano-Reggiano cheese

MAKES 4–6 SERVINGS

RECOMMENDED USES
Serve this Provençal-inspired recipe with panfried lamb chops or grilled tuna.

1 Prepare the fennel

If you are new to working with fennel, turn to page 41. Using a chef's knife, trim off the stalks and feathery tops, or *fronds*, of the fennel bulbs. Set aside some of the fronds. Run a vegetable peeler over the outer layer of the bulbs to remove any bruised or tough portions. (If the outer layer is badly bruised or scarred, pull off the entire portion.) Cut each of the bulbs in half from top to bottom, cutting right through the core. Cut each half lengthwise into 4 wedges, also going through the core to keep the layers joined together. Set aside. Rinse the fronds and dry well. Separate the fronds from their stems and gather the fronds into a pile on the cutting board. Using the chef's knife, rock the blade up and down and back and forth over the fronds until they are evenly chopped into very fine pieces, or *minced*. Measure out 1 tablespoon of the minced fronds and set aside; you'll use them later for garnish.

2 Prepare the tomatoes

Using a chef's knife, cut the tomatoes in half crosswise through their equators. Working with 1 half at a time and using the large holes of a box grater-shredder, grate the tomatoes into a bowl. It's fine to include the peels and seeds. You should have about ½ cup (⅓ lb/155 g) grated tomato.

3 Mince the garlic

For more details on working with garlic, turn to page 32. Place the cloves on a cutting board, press against them firmly with the flat side of the chef's knife, and peel away the papery skin. Cut the cloves in half lengthwise and then thinly slice each half lengthwise. Gather the slices in a small pile and rock the blade of the knife over the slices until coarsely chopped. Clean off any bits of garlic from the knife, gather the pieces into a compact pile, and continue to chop until the garlic pieces are very fine, or *minced*. You should have about 1½ teaspoons minced garlic.

4 Cook the garlic, wine, and tomato

Place a wide, shallow nonreactive sauté pan with a tight-fitting lid over medium heat and add the olive oil. When the surface of the oil appears to shimmer, it is sufficiently hot. Add the garlic and cook, stirring frequently, until softened, about 1 minute. Add the wine and grated tomato and bring to a boil. As soon as you see large bubbles begin to form, reduce the heat until only small bubbles occasionally break the surface, and simmer until the liquid is reduced by one-third, about 4 minutes. ›

5 Toast and grind the fennel seeds

While the tomato mixture is reducing, toast and grind the fennel seeds. If you need help toasting the seeds, turn to page 36. First, place a small, dry small frying pan over medium heat. Add the fennel seeds and toast, stirring frequently, until fragrant, about 2½ minutes. Immediately transfer the seeds to a plate to cool. Next, place the seeds in a spice grinder or a small electric coffee mill reserved only for spices and process until finely ground. (Alternatively, grind the seeds in a mortar with a pestle.)

6 Braise the fennel

Preheat the oven to 200°F (95°C) and place a serving dish in the oven to warm. Add the fennel wedges, ground fennel seeds, chicken stock, and salt to the pan with the tomato mixture and stir to combine. Raise the heat to high and bring to a boil. As soon as you see large bubbles begin to form, reduce the heat to low, cover the pan, and simmer until the fennel is somewhat tender but still offers resistance when pierced with the tip of a paring knife, about 15 minutes. Uncover, raise the heat to medium-high, and cook until the liquid is reduced to about 2 tablespoons and the fennel is tender all the way through when pierced, 4–5 minutes longer.

7 Grate the cheese

Parmigiano-Reggiano is a hard cheese designed for grating. It will always taste best if you freshly grate it just before using. While the fennel is braising, use the small grating holes of a box grater-shredder or a rasp cheese grater to grate the cheese. Set it aside in a small bowl.

8 Serve the fennel

Transfer the braised fennel to the warmed serving dish and sprinkle with the minced fennel fronds. You won't need to adjust the seasonings before serving; the Parmigiano-Reggiano cheese will add saltiness when sprinkled over the top. Serve right away and pass the cheese at the table for diners to add as they like.

CHEF'S TIP

When reducing liquid in a pan, first tip the pan to collect the liquid in a corner. This lets you know how much you have at the beginning. Then, as the liquid reduces, tip the pan occasionally to see if the liquid has reduced by one-half, one-third, or a similar measurement. It's much easier to judge the amount of liquid left when the pan is tipped.

Braised Vegetable Variations

Now that you've mastered Braised Fennel with White Wine & Tomato (page 70), you can use this same technique of slow cooking in moist heat to prepare other vegetables. Here are just three examples: Celery, usually thought of as a crisp vegetable, becomes meltingly tender and succulent in a braising liquid laced with lemon and thyme and finished with butter. Braised leeks, served with a robust vinaigrette flavored with mustard, shallots, and tarragon, show how you can braise vegetables in the oven as well as on top of the stove. Finally, endives are converted from a familiar salad green to a rich, cream-based braise worthy of a special meal. Each variation makes 4 to 6 servings.

Celery with Lemon & Thyme

Celery loses its signature crispness in this herb-scented braise.

Peel the tough outer strings along the curved edges of the stalks of **1 bunch celery**. Set aside some of the celery leaves. Cut the stalks into sections about 4 inches (10 cm) long. Chop enough celery leaves to yield 2 tablespoons.

In a sauté pan over medium-high heat, combine **1½ cups (12 fl oz/375 ml) chicken stock, ¼ cup (1 oz/30 g) finely diced yellow onion, 1 sprig fresh thyme,** and **1 strip lemon zest (about 2 inches/5 cm long)**. Bring to a boil, reduce the heat to medium-low, and simmer until reduced to ¾ cup (6 fl oz/180 ml), about 5 minutes. Add **1 tablespoon unsalted butter** and **⅛ teaspoon sea salt** and stir until the butter melts. Add the celery pieces, putting the thicker ones on the bottom. Cover and simmer until the celery is tender, about 15 minutes. Transfer the celery to a warmed platter, leaving the liquid in the pan.

Add **2 teaspoons unsalted butter**, the chopped celery leaves, **1 teaspoon fresh lemon juice,** and **⅛ teaspoon freshly ground pepper** to the liquid, raise the heat to high, and boil for 1 minute. Pour over the celery and serve right away.

Leeks with Mustard Sauce

These leeks are a typical first course on menus in French bistros.

Preheat the oven to 375°F (190°C). Lightly butter or oil a 9-by-12-inch (23-by-30-cm) baking dish.

Cut off the tough green parts and trim the roots of **4–6 long, thick leeks,** keeping the root ends intact. Halve the leeks lengthwise and rinse thoroughly.

Arrange the leeks, cut side up, in the prepared dish and sprinkle with **¼ teaspoon sea salt**. Pour **2½ cups (20 fl oz/625 ml) warmed chicken stock** over the leeks, adding just enough to cover the tops. Cover with parchment (baking) paper and oven-braise until the leeks are tender, about 25 minutes.

Meanwhile, in a small bowl, stir together **2 tablespoons finely diced shallots, 1½ tablespoons red wine vinegar,** and **⅛ teaspoon sea salt**. Let stand for 5 minutes, then whisk in **3 tablespoons *each* extra-virgin olive oil and crème fraîche, 2 teaspoons Dijon mustard,** and **1 tablespoon minced fresh tarragon**.

Transfer the leeks to a warmed platter, shaking off any excess liquid. Whisk the sauce, spoon over the leeks, and serve right away.

Endives with Cream Sauce

When cooked, endives develop a flavor imbued with nutty overtones. The addition of cream and tarragon makes them succulent and aromatic.

Trim the bases of **6 plump heads Belgian endive (chicory/witloof), about 1¾–2 lb (875 g–1 kg) total weight**. Halve the endives lengthwise.

In a sauté pan over medium-high heat, melt **3 tablespoons unsalted butter**. Add the endives, cut sides down, and cook until the cut sides are lightly golden, 4–5 minutes. Using tongs, gently turn the endives over and sprinkle with **½ teaspoon sea salt** and **⅛ teaspoon freshly ground white pepper**. Add **⅓ cup (3 fl oz/80 ml) chicken stock** and bring to a boil. Cover the pan, reduce the heat to low, and cook until the endives are tender, about 20 minutes.

Add **⅔ cup (5 fl oz/160 ml) heavy (double) cream,** then sprinkle with **2 teaspoons chopped fresh tarragon** and **1 teaspoon fresh lemon juice**. Raise the heat to medium and continue to cook, shaking the pan gently from time to time, until the cream has reduced to a thick sauce, about 5 minutes. Transfer the endives to a warmed serving dish, pour the sauce over the top, and serve right away.

Maple-Glazed Carrots with Shallots & Parsley

In this technique, a modified form of braising, carrots are cooked at a higher heat to reduce the liquid to a light, thin, pleasingly sweet glaze. Here, maple syrup is used to complement the natural sweetness of the carrots and contribute to the sheen and coating qualities of the glaze. The shallots and parsley add bite and contrast.

1 Prepare the carrots

Carrots are prepared differently depending on their size. Small garden carrots can be left whole, slightly larger ones are often cut into 3-inch (7.5-cm) sections, and large carrots are usually thinly sliced. Whichever size carrots you use, remove their skins with a vegetable peeler. Switch to a chef's knife and trim off the leafy tops and rootlike ends, if present. If using large carrots, cut them on the diagonal into even slices about ⅜ inch (1 cm) thick. In every case, make sure that the carrots are all about the same size so that they will cook at the same rate.

2 Finely dice the shallots

If you are not sure how to dice a shallot, turn to page 31. Using a paring knife, cut the shallots in half lengthwise and peel each half. One at a time, place the shallot halves, cut side down, on the cutting board. Makes a series of parallel vertical cuts, being sure to stop just short of the root end (this holds the shallot half together as you cut). Then make a series of parallel horizontal cuts and finally crosswise cuts to create ⅛-inch (3-mm) dice.

3 Cook the shallots

Preheat the oven to 200°F (95°C) and place a serving dish in the oven to warm. Place a wide, shallow sauté pan with a tight-fitting lid over medium heat and add 1 tablespoon of the butter. When the butter has melted and the foam begins to subside, add the diced shallots. Stir with a wooden spoon to coat the shallots evenly with the butter and cook, stirring often, for 1 minute.

4 Braise the carrots

Add the carrots, salt, and pepper to the pan with the shallots. Raise the heat to high and stir the carrots to coat evenly. Drizzle the maple syrup over the carrots and add the chicken stock. The liquid should come about halfway up the sides of the carrots. If it doesn't, add more stock or water as needed. Bring the liquid to a boil, reduce the heat to medium-high to maintain a lively but not fierce boil, and cover the pan. The aim is to reduce the liquid to a thin coating, or *glaze*, by the time the carrots are done cooking. ›

1½ lb (750 g) carrots

2 large shallots

2 tablespoons unsalted butter

½ teaspoon sea salt

¼ teaspoon freshly ground pepper

2½ tablespoons maple syrup

1 cup (8 fl oz/250 ml) chicken stock or canned low-sodium chicken broth, plus extra if needed for the braising liquid

6–8 sprigs fresh flat-leaf (Italian) parsley

MAKES 4–6 SERVINGS

CHEF'S TIP

When measuring sticky ingredients such as maple syrup, lightly coat the spoon with oil first. The sticky liquid will slip out easily and cleanly.

5 Chop the parsley

While the carrots are cooking, chop the parsley. If you need help chopping small leafy herbs, turn to page 34. Pluck the leaves from the parsley sprigs and discard the stems. Gather the leaves in a small pile on the cutting board. With the fingertips of one hand resting on top of the tip of the chef's knife, rock the blade up and down and back and forth over the leaves until they are uniformly chopped into coarse pieces. Measure out 1 tablespoon of the chopped parsley.

6 Test for doneness

After the carrots have cooked for about 5 minutes, check them for doneness by piercing a few pieces with the tip of a paring knife. They should be somewhat tender but still offer some resistance.

7 Reduce the liquid to a glaze

At this point, there should be about ½ cup (4 fl oz/125 ml) liquid remaining in the pan. Raise the heat to high and boil, uncovered, until the liquid has reduced to just a tablespoon or so, cloaking the carrots with a thin but shiny glaze, 3–4 minutes. Once the liquid has reduced, add the remaining 1 tablespoon butter and cook, turning the carrots with a wooden spoon to coat them thoroughly with the shiny glaze, for 1–2 minutes longer. The carrots should now be tender; be careful not to let them overcook.

8 Adjust the seasonings and serve

Taste the carrots and adjust the seasonings, adding a bit more salt or pepper if desired to suit your taste. Finally, toss the carrots with the parsley, transfer to the warmed serving dish, and serve right away.

CHEF'S TIP

For an eye-catching side dish, try using carrots in a variety of colors—snow white, pale yellow, deep red. You'll find them at farmers' markets in the spring and then again in autumn.

Glazed Vegetable Variations

Maple-Glazed Carrots with Shallots & Parsley (page 75) has taught you how to braise vegetables over relatively high heat with a little maple syrup, creating a light glaze that delivers an attractive sheen and a mildly sweet taste. Here are three variations on this technique. Despite their sturdy appearance, you can easily overcook parsnips, which is why the braising process must be interrupted, whereas beets are steamed until tender before they are braised. The sweetener can vary, too, with honey replacing the maple syrup, while such ingredients as mustard, orange juice, or vinegar are added to temper the final sweetness of the dish. Each variation makes 4 to 6 servings.

Mustard-Glazed Parsnips

Two types of mustard temper the natural sweetness of parsnips.

Peel 1¾–2 lb (875 g–1 kg) parsnips and cut them into pieces about 1½ inches (4 cm) long. Halve or quarter the large ends and middle pieces. Using a paring knife, remove the cores from the halved and quartered sections.

In a sauté pan, combine the parsnips, 1 cup (8 fl oz/250 ml) chicken stock, 4 teaspoons maple syrup, 1 tablespoon unsalted butter, ½ teaspoon sea salt, and ¼ teaspoon freshly ground white pepper. Bring to a boil over medium-high heat. Cover, reduce the heat to medium-low, and simmer until the parsnips are tender yet firm, 5–7 minutes. Remove from the heat.

Using a slotted spoon, transfer the parsnips to a bowl. Whisk 1 teaspoon *each* Dijon mustard and whole-grain mustard into the cooking liquid and return to medium heat. Simmer until the liquid is reduced to 3 tablespoons glaze, about 3 minutes. Return the parsnips to the pan and cook, turning often to coat with the glaze, until tender, about 3 minutes longer. Taste and adjust the seasonings. Transfer to a warmed serving dish and serve right away.

Glazed Pearl Onions with Rosemary

Here, a rosemary-scented glaze cloaks each small onion.

Bring a saucepan three-fourths full of water to a boil. Add 1 lb (500 g) red or white pearl onions and boil for 1 minute. Drain and run under running cold water to cool. Trim away the small root ends and slip the onions from their skins.

In a sauté pan over medium heat, melt 2 tablespoons unsalted butter. Stir in the onions. Raise the heat to medium-high and cook, stirring often, until they start to brown, about 5 minutes. Add ¼ teaspoon sea salt, 1 teaspoon minced fresh rosemary, 1 tablespoon honey, and 1 cup (8 fl oz/250 ml) chicken stock. Cover the pan and cook until the stock has nearly evaporated and the onions are tender, about 10 minutes.

Raise the heat to medium-high, stir in 1 tablespoon balsamic vinegar and ⅛ teaspoon freshly ground pepper, and cook until the liquid has reduced to 1 tablespoon glaze, about 1 minute. Toss the onions with the glaze. Taste and adjust the seasonings. Transfer to a warmed serving dish and serve right away.

Beets Glazed with Honey, Orange & Clove

Whether red, golden, or striped, beets can be first steamed to near tenderness, then quickly braised to a finish with this orange-scented glaze.

Cut all but 1 inch (2.5 cm) of the stems from 4–6 beets (about 1½ lb/750 g total weight). Rinse the beets well and steam until tender, 25–40 minutes (see page 57). One at a time, rinse the beets and slip off their skins, using a paring knife if needed. Trim away the stem and root ends. Cut into wedges or chunks.

In a sauté pan over medium heat, melt 1 tablespoon unsalted butter. Add the beets along with 1 teaspoon grated orange zest, ¾ cup (6 fl oz/180 ml) fresh orange juice, 2 teaspoons orange-blossom honey, ¼ teaspoon sea salt, ⅛ teaspoon freshly ground pepper, and 2 whole cloves. Bring to a lively simmer over medium-high heat and cook, shaking the beets around in the pan, until they are heated through and the liquid has reduced to 3 tablespoons glaze, about 6 minutes. Stir to coat the beets with the glaze. Taste and adjust the seasonings. Sprinkle with 1 teaspoon chopped fresh flat-leaf (Italian) parsley, transfer to a warmed serving dish, and serve right away.

Quick Braise of Spring Peas with Red Onion Shoots

In this seasonal dish, two springtime harvests, bright green English peas and scarlet-hued onion shoots are paired in a fresh-tasting side dish. Both vegetables are delicate, which means that the braise cooks so quickly that the pan doesn't need to be covered. The last-minute addition of basil contributes a mild anise note.

1 Sliver the basil
Preheat the oven to 200°F (95°C) and place a serving bowl in the oven to warm. If you need help slivering large leafy herbs, turn to page 36. Working in 2 batches, stack the basil leaves on top of one another. Roll the stack of leaves lengthwise as tightly as possible into a cylinder. Using a chef's knife, cut the leaves crosswise, which will create thin slivers. These slivers are known as a *chiffonade*. Measure out 2 tablespoons of the slivered basil. Set aside.

2 Prepare the onions
Red onion shoots are treated just like green onions. For more details on how to work with them, turn to page 33. Using the chef's knife, trim off the root ends and tough green tops of the onions. Line up the onions and cut the red (or white) parts and about 1 inch (2.5 cm) of the tender green parts crosswise into thin slices. Reserve the remaining green parts for another use.

3 Shell the peas
Remove the peas from their pods, or *shell* them, just before cooking so that they don't dry out. Have ready a bowl. Working with 1 pod at a time, pinch the tip at each end to begin splitting the pod. Squeeze the pod, pressing your thumb against the seam to continue opening it. Sweep your thumb down along the inside of the pod to pop out the peas from the pod and let them fall into the bowl. Discard the pod.

4 Cook the onions
In a wide, shallow sauté pan over medium-high heat, melt 1 tablespoon of the butter. Add the onions, stir with a wooden spoon to coat them evenly with the butter, and cook, stirring once or twice, until softened, about 1 minute.

5 Simmer the peas
Add the chicken stock, peas, and salt to the pan and stir to combine. Bring to a boil, then reduce the heat to medium and simmer until the peas are heated through and the onions are tender, 3–4 minutes. Remove from the heat and stir in the remaining 1 tablespoon butter, the pepper, and the basil.

6 Adjust the seasonings and serve
Taste and adjust the seasonings, adding more salt or pepper if desired to suit your taste. Transfer to the warmed serving bowl and serve right away.

12–16 leaves fresh basil

1 bunch red onion shoots or green (spring) onions

3 lb (1.5 kg) English peas in their pods

2 tablespoons unsalted butter

¾ cup (6 fl oz/180 ml) chicken stock, canned low-sodium chicken broth, or water

¼ teaspoon sea salt

⅛ teaspoon freshly ground pepper

MAKES 4–6 SERVINGS

CHEF'S TIP
Peas are only in season in the spring before the weather turns hot. If they are not available, you can use frozen peas to make this dish. Simply substitute 3 cups (1 lb/500 g) frozen petite peas for the fresh ones.

RECOMMENDED USES
Serve with the first wild salmon of the season or with halibut. If using fresh peas, consider serving the braise as a first course.

Red Cabbage Braised with Bacon & Apples

This traditional braised cabbage dish can hold its own among more contemporary recipes with its sweet-sour tang and silky, succulent texture. Bacon gives the dish a smoky accent, while vinegar and apples add their bright flavors. The vinegar also keeps the cabbage appealingly firm as it braises.

1 red cabbage, about 2 lb (1 kg)

2 tart apples such as Pink Lady

1 small red onion

3 slices smoked bacon, diced (page 37)

1 tablespoon canola oil, if needed to supplement the bacon fat

1½ teaspoons sea salt

¼ teaspoon freshly ground pepper

6 tablespoons unrefined cider vinegar

3 tablespoons firmly packed brown sugar

MAKES 4–6 SERVINGS

CHEF'S TIP

This recipe is a perfect example of the usefulness of mise en place. *Once all the ingredients are chopped and measured, everything goes into the pot at pretty much the same time. They then cook, their flavors developing and mingling, with little additional effort from the cook.*

1 **Prepare the cabbage**
If you need help working with cabbage, turn to page 39. Remove any bruised or wilted outer leaves from the cabbage. Cut it into quarters through the core, and cut out the hard inner core from each quarter. Cut each quarter crosswise into slices about ¼ inch (6 mm) wide. Plunge the sliced cabbage into a bowl of cold water, then drain in a colander, but don't dry it; you want some water clinging to the leaves when they go into the pot. Set the cabbage aside.

2 **Prepare the apples and onion**
Using a chef's knife, cut the apples into quarters and cut away the cores. Chop the quarters finely and set aside. Cut the onion in half lengthwise through the root end and peel each half. One at a time, place the onion halves, cut side down, on the cutting board and cut each half crosswise into thin slices.

3 **Cook the bacon**
Place a 6-qt (6-l) stainless-steel or enameled cast-iron Dutch oven (other materials will react with red cabbage, turning it an unappetizing color) over medium heat. When the pan is hot, add the bacon. Cook, stirring occasionally, until the bacon is browned and its fat is melted, 4–5 minutes.

4 **Braise the ingredients**
When the bacon is done, if there is less than a tablespoon of fat in the pot, add the oil as needed to total 1 tablespoon. If the bacon has yielded more than a tablespoon of fat, remove from the heat, tip the pot, spoon off and discard all but 1 tablespoon, and return the pot to medium heat. (Don't pour the bacon fat down the drain, as it can cause clogs.) Add the cabbage, apples, and onion. Sprinkle with the salt and pepper and, using 2 wooden spoons, toss everything together as if tossing a salad. Add the vinegar and brown sugar, and toss again. Reduce the heat to low and cover the pan. Cook slowly, stirring once or twice, until the cabbage has wilted down considerably and is a soft, rather than a bright, purple, about 1 hour. Toward the end of the cooking time, preheat the oven to 200°F (95°C) and place a serving dish in the oven to warm.

5 **Adjust the seasonings and serve**
Taste the dish and adjust the seasonings, adding more salt, sugar, or vinegar a little at a time until you reach a flavor balance you like. Transfer the cabbage to the warmed serving dish and serve right away.

Braised Mushrooms with Sherry & Cream

You can use any combination of fresh mushrooms you like in this savory braise, keeping in mind that a mixture of colors and shapes is critical to visual appeal. The marriage of mushrooms and sherry, a fortified wine, is hardly a new one—they are highly compatible, with the sherry enriching the mushrooms' woodsy flavors.

1 Soak the dried mushrooms
Place the dried mushrooms in a heatproof bowl. Add the boiling water and let soak until softened, about 30 minutes. Drain the mushrooms through a sieve lined with a double layer of cheesecloth (muslin) set over a bowl, gently pressing against them to force out the liquid. Reserve the liquid. If you used porcini, chop coarsely. If you used morels, halve lengthwise. Set the mushrooms aside.

2 Prepare the fresh mushrooms
For more details on preparing fresh mushrooms, turn to page 43. Using a mushroom brush, gently brush away any dirt from the mushrooms, or wipe with a damp paper towel. Using a paring knife, trim a thin slice from the base of the stem of each button and cremini mushroom, if using, and discard. If the stems are very tough, remove them completely. If using portobellos, cut off and discard the stems, scrape out the gills, and then cut the caps into wedges. Cut off and discard the entire stem of each shiitake. Cut the button, cremini, and shiitake mushrooms into halves or quarters, depending on their size, to make fairly large chunks, about ¾ inch (2 cm). Oyster mushrooms can be left whole or cut lengthwise into slices ¾ inch (2 cm) thick if very large.

3 Cook the shallots and the firm mushrooms
In a wide, shallow sauté pan with a tight-fitting lid, melt 3 tablespoons of the butter over medium-high heat. Add the shallots and soaked dried mushrooms and stir with a wooden spoon to coat evenly with the butter. Cook, stirring often, for 1 minute. Raise the heat to high and add the button, cremini or portobello, and shiitake mushrooms. Add ½ teaspoon of the salt and the pepper and cook, stirring often, until the mushrooms begin to release their juices, about 5 minutes.

4 Add the oyster mushrooms and make the sauce
Add the garlic, the reserved mushroom-soaking liquid, and the remaining 1 tablespoon butter and ½ teaspoon salt and stir to combine. Reduce the heat to medium, cover the pan, and let simmer for 10 minutes. Gently stir in the oyster mushrooms, re-cover the pan, and cook until nearly tender, about 2 minutes. Add the sherry and cream and cook until slightly reduced, about 2 minutes longer.

5 Adjust the seasonings and serve
Taste and adjust the seasonings, adding more salt and pepper if desired to suit your taste. Sprinkle with the parsley and serve right away.

½ cup (½ oz/15 g) dried porcini or morel mushrooms

1½ cups (12 fl oz/375 ml) boiling water

½ lb (250 g) fresh brown or white button mushrooms

6 oz (185 g) cremini or portobello mushrooms

6 oz (185 g) fresh oyster mushrooms

¼ lb (125 g) fresh shiitake mushrooms

4 tablespoons (2 oz/60 g) unsalted butter

⅓ cup (1½ oz/45 g) finely diced shallots (page 31)

1 teaspoon sea salt

¼ teaspoon freshly ground pepper

¼ teaspoon minced garlic (page 32)

2 tablespoons dry sherry

¼ cup (2 fl oz/60 ml) heavy (double) cream

1 tablespoon chopped fresh flat-leaf (Italian) parsley or tarragon (page 34)

MAKES 4–6 SERVINGS

> **RECOMMENDED USES**
> *Serve these classic mushrooms on toasted bread (shown here with crostini), or alongside scrambled eggs, soufflés, pasta, or polenta.*

2 slices bacon, diced (page 37)

1 tablespoon unsalted butter

1 small or medium yellow onion, finely diced
(page 30)

1–1½ lb (500–750 g) Brussels sprouts

¾ cup (6 fl oz/180 ml) chicken stock, canned
low-sodium chicken broth, or water

¾ teaspoon sea salt

¼ teaspoon freshly ground pepper

MAKES 4–6 SERVINGS

 CHEF'S TIP
*To cut up slices of bacon quickly, you
can use kitchen scissors. They make
quick work of snipping the bacon into
small pieces.*

Braised Brussels Sprouts with Bacon & Onion

The approach here uses two cooking methods, steaming the Brussels sprouts first
before braising them with bacon and onions in a small amount of liquid. While the
sprouts may lose some of their green crispness, the fusion of flavors that results
from this last bit of braising is what makes them so tasty.

1 Cook the bacon
Preheat the oven to 200°F (95°C) and place a serving dish in the oven to
warm. Place a wide, shallow sauté pan with a tight-fitting lid over medium heat.
When the pan is hot, add the bacon and cook, stirring occasionally, until lightly
browned but not fully crisped, about 5 minutes. Tip the pan and spoon off and
discard all but 1 tablespoon of the fat and add the butter. When the butter has
melted, add the onion and stir with a wooden spoon to coat the onion evenly with
the fat and butter. Reduce the heat to low and cook, stirring occasionally to
prevent sticking, until golden, 3–4 minutes. Remove the pan from the heat.

2 Trim and steam the Brussels sprouts
For more details on steaming vegetables, see page 20. Set a steamer basket or
steamer insert in a saucepan. Add water to come just up to the bottom of the
steamer and bring to a boil. While the water is heating, trim the Brussels sprouts.
If you need help, turn to page 42. Using a paring knife, trim the stem end of each
Brussels sprout and remove any withered or yellowed leaves. Cut any larger sprouts
into halves or quarters through the core to make them about the same size as the
smallest ones. It's a good idea to cut even smallish Brussels sprouts in half. They
cook more quickly and the cuts reveal crevices in the layers of leaves that nicely
trap the onion and bacon. Add the trimmed Brussels sprouts to the steamer basket,
distributing them evenly. Reduce the heat to medium, cover the pan, and steam
until the sprouts are somewhat tender but still offer resistance when pierced with
the tip of the paring knife, 8–10 minutes.

3 Deglaze the pan and braise the Brussels sprouts
Using an oven mitt to protect your hand, grip the handle of the steamer
basket or steamer insert and lift it out of the pan. Carefully shake it to release any
excess water, and add the Brussels sprouts to the pan with the bacon and onion.
Return the pan to the medium heat and stir in the chicken stock, scraping the
bottom of the pan with a wooden spoon to loosen any browned bits; this is called
deglazing the pan. These browned bits add flavor to the final sauce. Add the salt
and pepper, cover, and simmer until fully tender and fragrant, about 5 minutes.

4 Adjust the seasonings and serve
Taste and adjust the seasonings, adding more salt or pepper a little at a time
to suit your taste. Transfer to the warmed serving bowl and serve right away.

5

Sautéed & Stir-fried Vegetables

Sautéing and stir-frying, both done over high heat, are two of the fastest ways you can cook, and both impart a special flavor and rich color to vegetables. Advance preparation pays off. You add ingredients quickly in both methods, so they must all be ready to go. You will also learn how to sear vegetables first in a small amount of hot fat, and then how to toss them in the pan to cook them evenly.

Stir-fried Spring Vegetables with Ginger, Lemon & Mint

In this recipe, seasonings typical in the West—lemon and mint—combine with ginger, a traditional ingredient of the East, to bring out the bright, fresh flavors of the spring vegetables. The stir-fry technique of quick tossing over high heat releases the essence of the asparagus and peas while preserving their crispness.

1 Prepare the asparagus

If needed, pat the asparagus dry with a kitchen towel. Not all asparagus should be prepared the same way. Thicker spears must be trimmed and then peeled to make them more succulent, while thin spears need only be snapped to remove their tough ends. If you are using thick asparagus, use a chef's knife to cut away the bottom of each spear where it starts to change color, becoming paler and visibly tougher. Discard the ends. Using a vegetable peeler, peel the outer green skin from each thick spear to within about 2 inches (5 cm) of the tip. (Alternatively, if you are using thin asparagus—about the width of a pencil—lightly hold a spear with your fingers and begin bending it at the end opposite the tip until it breaks naturally; the spear will snap precisely where the fibrous, tough, paler inedible portion begins. Discard the ends. You don't need to peel thin spears.)

2 Cut the asparagus into pieces

Put the thick or thin spears on a cutting board. Working with 1 spear at a time and using a chef's knife, cut each spear crosswise on the diagonal into 2-inch (5-cm) pieces. Put the asparagus pieces in a bowl and place them near the stove so you can easily reach them.

3 Prepare the sugar snap and snow peas

If needed, pat the peas dry with a kitchen towel. Typically sugar snap peas are sold with a small stem and/or tiny leaves attached, while snow peas are usually stem free. Pinch off and discard the stems of the sugar snap peas and of the snow peas, if present. Most edible pod peas today are string free, but if there are any strings on the peas, pull them off and discard. For a more decorative look, trim the stem end of each pea pod with a diagonal cut using the chef's knife. Put the peas in separate bowls and place them near the stove. ❯

1 lb (500 g) thick or thin asparagus spears

⅓ lb (155 g) sugar snap peas

¼ lb (125 g) snow peas (mangetouts)

2 green (spring) onions

2-inch (5-cm) piece fresh ginger

1 or 2 lemons

12–16 leaves fresh mint, plus small leaves or sprigs for garnish

2 tablespoons peanut or grapeseed oil

¾ teaspoon sea salt

Light soy sauce for seasoning, optional

MAKES 4–6 SERVINGS

CHEF'S TIP

When stir-frying or sautéing, it's best to dry the vegetables well after rinsing. If you add them to the pan while they're still wet, they won't sear properly and they will splatter and steam in the residual water.

4 Prepare the green onions

For more details on working with green onions, turn to page 33. Using the chef's knife, trim off the root ends and tough green tops of the onions. Line up the onions and cut them crosswise on the diagonal into thin slices. Place them in a bowl near the stove.

5 Mince the ginger

Using a paring knife, remove the thin beige skin from the ginger. Then use the chef's knife to cut it into coin-shaped slices. Cut the slices into narrow strips, and cut the strips crosswise into small pieces. Gather the pieces into a pile, and rock the heel of the knife blade up and down and back and forth over the pieces. Measure out 1½ tablespoons minced ginger and place in a bowl near the stove.

6 Zest the lemon(s)

To find out more about zesting citrus, turn to page 38. Using a fine rasp grater, remove the colored part of the peel from the lemon(s), taking care not to grate the bitter white pith underneath. Measure out 1 tablespoon grated zest and place in a bowl near the stove. Reserve the lemon(s) for another use.

7 Sliver the mint

If you need help slivering large leafy herbs, turn to page 36. Working in 2 batches, stack the mint leaves on top of one another. Roll the stack of leaves lengthwise into a tight cylinder. Using the chef's knife, cut the leaves crosswise, which will create thin slivers. Measure out 2 tablespoons slivered mint and add it to the bowl with the green onions.

8 Ready your equipment

Make sure you have all your equipment ready, as you will need to cook the dish quickly. Preheat the oven to 200°F (95°C) and place a serving bowl or platter in the oven to warm. Have ready a wok, preferably about 14 inches (35 cm) in diameter, and 2 long-handled wooden spoons or spatulas. Stir-frying can generate smoke, so be sure to turn on your kitchen ventilation to circulate the air. ⟩

CHEF'S TIP

Be sure to have all of your vegetables and seasonings trimmed, sliced, and within easy reach of the stove before heating the wok. Stir-frying goes so quickly that there is no time to prepare ingredients once you've begun.

9 Heat the wok

Place the wok over high heat and let it stand for a minute or two. When stir-frying, it's important to preheat the wok until it is as hot as possible. Hold your hand over the pan until you feel heat rising, then add the peanut oil. Carefully tilt and rotate the pan so that the oil is distributed evenly over the surface. Allow the oil to heat briefly until it is hot and shimmering.

CHEF'S TIP

Another way to test the wok to see if it is hot enough to add the oil and begin stir-frying is to flick a drop of water into the pan. If the drop sizzles on contact, the wok is ready.

10 Begin to stir-fry

For this stir-fry, you add the vegetables in the order of their cooking time, from longest to shortest. First, add the asparagus and ½ teaspoon of the salt and cook, tossing and stirring constantly with the 2 wooden spoons or spatulas, for about 1 minute. Next, add the ginger and sugar snap peas and cook, again tossing and stirring constantly, for another minute. Now, add the snow peas and the remaining ¼ teaspoon salt and toss and stir until the snow peas are bright green and tender on the outside but still slightly crisp in the center when you bite into one, about 30 seconds longer. Adding the vegetables at different intervals will ensure that they are all cooked at the same time.

11 Add the rest of the seasonings

Add the green onions, lemon zest, and mint and toss with the spatulas to combine them with the vegetables. You want to add these seasonings last so they stay fresh and bright.

12 Adjust the seasonings and serve

Taste and adjust the seasonings, adding a little more salt or a few drops of soy sauce (which is also salty) if needed until you reach a flavor balance you like. Transfer the stir-fry to the warmed serving bowl or platter, garnish with the mint leaves or sprigs, and serve right away.

Serving ideas

The traditional accompaniment to stir-fries is steamed white rice. The bland, fluffy white grains contrast nicely with the bright flavor and crisp texture of the vegetables. Noodles work well for the same reason, their chewy texture countering the crunchy stir-fry. The rice or noodles take longer to cook than the vegetables, so have one or the other ready before you begin stir-frying. Protein-rich tofu is a third accompaniment option.

With white rice and ginger garnish (top left)
A fried ginger garnish adds flair to spring vegetables and white rice. Cut fresh ginger into fine slivers, then fry in ½ inch (12 mm) peanut oil until lightly browned, 20–30 seconds. Drain on paper towels.

With seared tofu (left)
Heat 2 tablespoons peanut oil in the empty pan. Add thin, 2-inch (5-cm) squares of firm tofu and sear, turning once, until golden on both sides, 5–7 minutes. Top with slivered green onion and soy sauce to taste.

With noodles (above)
Chinese egg noodles are also traditional with stir-fries. Boil the noodles, drain, and then divide among individual dishes, placing the vegetables on top.

Sautéed Peppers & Onion

Bell peppers come into their prime in late summer and early autumn. Red, orange, and yellow peppers look beautiful together, and searing them over high heat caramelizes some of their sweet juices and gives them a deep flavor. Red onion, also sweet and colorful, complements the peppers, while marjoram adds an herbal note.

1 Prepare the peppers

Preheat the oven to 200°F (95°C) and place a serving platter in the oven to warm. Using a chef's knife, first cut off the stem end from each pepper. Use your fingers to pull out the stem and cluster of seeds. Then cut each pepper in half lengthwise; this will expose the white ribs, or membranes. Brush away any lingering seeds and then, using a paring knife, cut away and discard the white ribs. Turn the halves skin side up and press on the curved ends with your palm to flatten each half. Now turn each half over so the skin side is facing down (it's easier to cut into the flesh, which has some texture, than the smooth skin). Using the chef's knife, cut each half lengthwise into slices about ⅜ inch (1 cm) thick.

2 Prepare the onion

Using a chef's knife, cut the onion in half lengthwise through the root end and peel each half. One at a time, place the onion halves, cut side down, on the cutting board and cut each half lengthwise into strips about ⅜ inch (1 cm) wide.

3 Chop the marjoram

To find out more about chopping small branched herbs, turn to page 35. Gently run your thumb and index finger down the marjoram sprigs to remove the leaves and then discard the stems. Gather the leaves in a small pile on the cutting board. With the fingertips of one hand resting on top of the tip of the chef's knife, rock the blade up and down and back and forth over the leaves until they are uniformly chopped into coarse pieces. Measure out 1 tablespoon chopped marjoram and set aside.

4 Heat the pan and prepare to sauté

For more details on sautéing vegetables, turn to page 24. Place a large frying pan over high heat. Hold your hand over the pan until you feel heat rising, then add the olive oil and let it heat for several seconds. While the pan is heating, place all your ingredients near the stove. Sautéing is a quick method of cooking, so you'll want to have everything you need close at hand. As soon as the surface of the oil appears to shimmer, you are ready to sauté.

3 large red, yellow, or orange bell peppers (capsicums), or a combination, about 1½ lb (750 g) total weight

1 red onion

6–8 sprigs fresh marjoram or thyme

3 tablespoons olive oil

¾ teaspoon sea salt

¼ teaspoon freshly ground pepper

Balsamic vinegar, optional

Fresh lemon juice, optional

MAKES 4–6 SERVINGS

CHEF'S TIP
Bell peppers vary widely in size and shape. For ease of preparation, look for peppers that are all about the same size and have relatively straight sides.

5 Sauté the peppers and onion

Add the peppers and onion to the pan all at once and sprinkle with the salt and pepper. Begin to sauté the vegetables by moving the peppers and onion around in the pan briskly, either sliding the pan back and forth with little jerks to make the ingredients hop, or simply stirring them with a wooden spoon or silicone spatula. This is called *sautéing*, which is derived from the French verb *sauter*, "to jump." Continue to sauté the peppers and onion, tossing or stirring them every 30 seconds or so at first and then occasionally thereafter, until they are tender-crisp and singed along their edges, about 7 minutes. You don't want to stir the vegetables constantly; letting them have some contact with the hot pan will sear them and give them the special flavor that comes from high-heat cooking.

6 Let the peppers and onion cool

Add the marjoram and toss to combine, then turn off the heat and let the peppers and onion cool in the pan for at least 5 minutes before adjusting the seasonings. Flavors are often easier to detect and are fuller in dishes that are not searingly hot.

7 Adjust the seasonings

Taste and adjust the seasonings. If the dish tastes bland to you, add a pinch more salt or pepper. The peppers and onion should be sweet, but if the dish seems to need more sweetness, add a few drops of balsamic vinegar. If the dish seems sweet enough but lacks brightness, add a few drops of lemon juice instead.

8 Serve the peppers and onion

Transfer the peppers and onion to the warmed platter, arranging them so they are slightly mounded in the center. Serve right away.

CHEF'S TIP

For softer, more succulent peppers and onion, add ½ cup (4 fl oz/125 ml) dry white wine or water after sautéing them in step 5. Reduce the heat to medium-low, cover the pan, and let the peppers and onion cook until softened, about 5 minutes. Uncover the pan, add the marjoram, and toss to combine. Adjust the seasonings and serve.

Sautéed Vegetable Variations

Now that you've practiced the basic sauté technique by making Sautéed Peppers & Onion (page 95), you can cook a number of other spring and summer vegetables using your new knowledge. All of them are seared quickly over high heat in a pan that allows for rapid stirring, but a few fresh ideas are also introduced, including the addition of crisped bread crumbs to the zucchini, a mix of butter and olive oil instead of oil alone on the asparagus, and the use of white wine in the fennel, which delivers both a little acidity and the liquid necessary to make this sturdy vegetable tender. Each variation makes 4 to 6 servings.

Zucchini with Toasted Bread Crumbs

Use any mix of colorful zucchini here, from pale green to green-black to yellow to ridged heirlooms. Toasted bread crumbs add crunch to the dish.

Cut 5 or 6 zucchini (courgettes), about 1½ lb (750 g) total weight, lengthwise into quarters and then crosswise into ½-inch (12-mm) pieces.

Toss ⅓ cup (⅔ oz/20 g) fresh bread crumbs with 2 teaspoons olive oil and toast in a small frying pan over low heat until golden and crisp, about 10 minutes. Transfer to a small bowl. In another small bowl, mix ½ teaspoon minced garlic, 1 teaspoon grated lemon zest, and 2 tablespoons chopped fresh marjoram.

Heat a large frying pan over medium-high heat. When hot, add 2½ tablespoons olive oil and then the zucchini and toss to coat with the oil. Add ¼ teaspoon sea salt and sauté until the zucchini are golden in places and tender yet firm, about 8 minutes. Add the garlic-herb mixture and sauté for 2 minutes longer.

Remove from the heat. Taste and adjust the seasonings. Add the toasted bread crumbs and toss to mix. Serve right away.

Asparagus with Fresh Herbs

Asparagus is good sautéed and seasoned with basil, chervil, cilantro, or parsley. Choose an herb that goes with the rest of your menu.

Trim the pale, tough ends from 1½–2 lb (750 g–1 kg) thick asparagus spears, then peel them to within about 2 inches (5 cm) of the tips. Cut the stalks crosswise on the diagonal into slices ¼ inch (6 mm) thick.

Heat a large frying pan over high heat. When hot, add 1 tablespoon *each* unsalted butter and olive oil. When the butter has melted, add the asparagus and sprinkle with ¼ teaspoon sea salt. Sauté the asparagus until tender-crisp, up to 10 minutes. Start tasting often after 5 minutes to avoid overcooking.

Remove from the heat. Taste and adjust the seasonings. Add ⅛ teaspoon freshly ground pepper and 1 tablespoon slivered fresh basil or finely chopped fresh chervil, cilantro (fresh coriander), or flat-leaf (Italian) parsley and toss to combine. Serve right away.

Sautéed Fennel

Fennel is crunchy and has a light anise flavor when raw, but becomes caramelized and rich when sautéed. Olive oil, salt, pepper, and a bit of the minced fennel fronds are all you need to season it.

Trim off the stalks and feathery tops of 3 large (10 oz/315 g) fennel bulbs. Set aside some of the fronds. Peel away any bruised or tough outer portions, then cut each bulb in half from top to bottom, cutting through the core. Cut the halves lengthwise into slices about ¼ inch (6 mm) thick; the core will keep the layers together. Set aside. Mince enough fronds to yield 1 tablespoon.

Heat a large frying pan over high heat. When hot, add 2 tablespoons olive oil and then the fennel and sprinkle with ¾ teaspoon sea salt. Sauté the fennel for about 10 minutes, then add ⅓ cup (3 fl oz/80 ml) dry white wine or water. Continue sautéing until the fennel is golden and tender, 5–7 minutes longer.

Remove from the heat. Taste and adjust the salt. Add ¼ teaspoon freshly ground pepper and the minced fronds and toss to combine. Sprinkle with freshly grated Parmigiano-Reggiano cheese, if desired, and serve right away.

2 bunches spinach, about ¾ lb (375 g) each or 1½ lb (750 g) total weight

1 small clove garlic

1 tablespoon olive oil

¼ teaspoon sea salt

1 teaspoon fresh lemon juice (page 38)

MAKES 4–6 SERVINGS

CHEF'S TIP
A salad spinner makes quick work of rinsing and drying spinach as well as other leafy greens. If you don't have one, you can just as easily rinse the spinach in a large bowl of water. Transfer the rinsed leaves to a colander to drain off most of the water then use paper towels to pat them dry.

RECOMMENDED USES
Serve with grilled or poached fish. Spinach is also always good with soufflés or other egg-based dishes.

Sautéed Spinach with Garlic & Lemon

This is one of the fastest spinach dishes you can make. After rinsing, many greens are cooked with some of the water still clinging to their leaves, but the spinach in this recipe is dried. The leaves cook too quickly for the water to evaporate, and you don't want any water to dilute the garlic or olive oil. The garlic and lemon make the spinach sharper and more lively tasting.

1 **Stem the spinach**
For help with stemming and then rinsing greens, turn to page 40. Sort through the spinach and discard any yellowed or wilted leaves. Fold each leaf in half along the stem with the vein side facing out. Grasp the stem with your other hand and quickly tear it away to remove the coarse, tough part of the vein.

2 **Rinse the spinach**
Fill the bowl of a salad spinner with cold water. Place the spinner basket in the water and add the spinach. Swish the spinach with your hand to loosen any sand or grit from the leaves, which will fall to the bottom of the bowl. Lift the basket and repeat rinsing with fresh water as necessary until there is no sand or grit visible in the bottom of the bowl. Spinach can be very sandy, and even a few grains will ruin a dish. Once it's clean, spin the spinach dry. Preheat the oven to 200°F (95°C) and place a serving dish in the oven to warm.

3 **Mince the garlic**
For more details on working with garlic, turn to page 32. Place the garlic clove on a cutting board, firmly press against it with the flat side of a chef's knife, and pull away the papery skin. Cut the clove in half lengthwise, then thinly slice. Rock the knife over the slices until chopped very fine, or *minced*.

4 **Sauté the spinach**
Place a large frying pan over high heat. When the pan is hot, add the olive oil, tilt and rotate the pan to distribute the oil evenly, and let it heat for several seconds. Next, pile the spinach in the pan. It may seem like you are adding too much spinach to the pan all at once, but it will cook down quickly and significantly reduce in volume. Add the garlic and the salt; adding the garlic after the spinach protects it from the high heat, which prevents it from burning. Immediately toss the spinach with a pair of tongs or 2 large forks, as if tossing a salad. This ensures that all the leaves will cook at the same rate. Continue tossing until the spinach is bright green and wilted, about 3 minutes. Remove from the heat, add the lemon juice, and toss again.

5 **Adjust the seasonings and serve**
Taste the spinach and evaluate the seasonings, adding more salt or lemon juice a little at a time until you achieve a flavor balance you like. Transfer to the warmed serving dish and serve right away.

Sautéed Green Variations

Sautéed Spinach with Garlic & Lemon (page 98) shows how the flavor of greens, like other vegetables, is intensified by the high, dry heat of sautéing. Not all greens are sautéed the same way, however. Spinach cooks the most quickly and needs only a tiny bit of moisture, if any, to wilt. Chard, collard greens, kale, and most other greens take longer to cook, so water or stock is added to the pan after the initial sautéing to produce the steam needed to ensure that the greens become tender. Finally, some greens, like broccoli rabe, are first cooked in boiling water and then only very briefly sautéed. Each variation makes at least 4 and up to 6 servings.

Chard with Lemon

In this recipe, chard is first sautéed and then simmered, rendering it tender and flavorful. Because chard is so voluminous raw, you'll need to cook it in 2 batches.

Cut off and discard the stems from 2 bunches small, tender chard. You should have 16–20 small chard leaves, or about 8–12 cups (½–¾ lb/250–375 g) tightly packed leaves. Coarsely chop the leaves, then rinse in a salad spinner and spin dry.

Heat a large frying pan over high heat. When hot, add 2 tablespoons olive oil and then half of the chard and sprinkle with ½ teaspoon sea salt. Sauté until wilted, 2½–3 minutes. Add ⅓ cup (3 fl oz/80 ml) chicken stock or water and continue cooking until the leaves are tender, 1–2 minutes longer. Taste and adjust the seasonings.

Transfer the chard to a warmed serving dish and cover to keep warm. Repeat with the remaining chard, heating 2 tablespoons olive oil, sprinkling with ½ teaspoon sea salt, and adding ⅓ cup chicken stock or water. Add to the platter. Garnish with 4–6 lemon wedges (1 for each person) and serve right away.

Slivered Collards with Toasted Sesame Seeds

When sliced into narrow ribbons, typically dense collard greens can be sautéed successfully. Asian sesame oil lends the dish a warm, aromatic flavor.

Cut off and discard the stems from 2 bunches collard greens. You should have 12–16 collard leaves, or about 8–10 cups (8–10 oz/250–315 g) tightly packed leaves. Stack 4–6 of the leaves on top of one another and roll the stack lengthwise into a tight cylinder. Cut the leaves crosswise into narrow ribbons no more than ¼ inch (6 mm) wide. Rinse the leaves well in a bowl of cold water and drain.

Heat a large frying pan over medium-high heat. When hot, add 2 tablespoons olive oil and then ⅓ cup (1½ oz/45 g) finely diced red onion. Sauté for 1 minute, then add the collard greens, along with the water clinging to them, and sprinkle with ¼ teaspoon sea salt. Sauté until wilted and tender, 5–7 minutes.

Transfer the collard greens to a warmed serving dish. Toss with 2 teaspoons toasted black or white sesame seeds and 1 teaspoon Asian sesame oil. Taste and adjust the seasonings. Serve right away.

Broccoli Rabe with Red Pepper & Garlic

Broccoli rabe can be sautéed without precooking, but the flavor will be sharper and you will need to discard the stems. Blanching it first makes it tender and more mild.

Bring a large saucepan three-fourths full of water to a boil. Meanwhile, trim the ends of the stalks from 1 bunch broccoli rabe, about (1 lb/500 g). Either remove and discard or peel any large stalks with a vegetable peeler. Rinse the broccoli rabe well in a bowl of cold water.

Add 2½ teaspoons sea salt to the boiling water. Add the broccoli rabe, return to a boil, and cook until tender yet firm, about 3 minutes. Drain and set aside.

Heat a large frying pan over medium-high heat. When hot, add 3 tablespoons olive oil and then 1 coarsely chopped garlic clove. Cook, stirring often, until the garlic is lightly golden, 2–3 minutes. Raise the heat to high and add the broccoli rabe and ⅛ teaspoon red pepper flakes. Sauté until the broccoli rabe is heated through and tender. Remove from the heat. Taste and adjust the seasonings. Transfer to a warmed dish and garnish with 4–6 lemon wedges (1 for each person). Serve right away.

Black Kale with Red Onion & Bacon

The leaves of black kale (also called *cavolo nero* or Tuscan kale) are especially sturdy and dense, so here they are boiled before going into the pan. This way, the leaves become tender and retain their dark green gleam.

Bring a large saucepan three-fourths full of water to a boil. Cut off and discard the stems from 2 bunches black kale. You should have about 8 cups (½ lb/250 g) tightly packed leaves. Rinse the leaves well in a bowl of cold water and drain.

Heat a large frying pan over medium heat. When hot, add 2 slices diced bacon and cook until browned, about 4 minutes. Drain on a paper towel–lined plate. Pour off any bacon fat from the pan, add 2 tablespoons olive oil, and heat over medium heat. Add 1 cup (4 oz/125 g) diced red onion and ⅛ teaspoon red pepper flakes. Stir to coat the onion with the oil and cook, stirring occasionally, while you boil the kale.

Add 2 teaspoons sea salt to the boiling water and add the kale. Return to a boil and cook until tender, 6–8 minutes. Using tongs, transfer the leaves, along with the water clinging to them, to the pan with the onion. Add ¼ teaspoon sea salt and the bacon and toss to mix. Raise the heat to medium-high and sauté until the pan is dry and the kale is glossy. Taste and adjust the seasonings. Transfer to a warmed serving dish and serve right away.

Creamed Spinach with Basil

Spinach in cream sauce is a perennial favorite. Classically, the spinach is chopped finely, but larger pieces make an attractive presentation, too. Here, slivered basil lends a fresh flavor.

Pull off and discard the stems from 2 large bunches spinach, about 1 lb (500 g) each. Rinse the leaves in a bowl of cold water, changing the water as needed. Drain in a colander. Add the spinach, along with the water clinging to it, to a large frying pan over high heat. Sauté just long enough to wilt the greens, about 4 minutes. (You may need to do this in 2 batches.) Transfer the wilted spinach to the colander. Using a silicone spatula, press out any excess water. Leave the leaves in large pieces or transfer to a cutting board and chop the leaves coarsely.

Heat a large saucepan over medium heat. When hot, add 4 teaspoons unsalted butter. When the butter has melted, add 3 tablespoons minced shallot. Cook, stirring often, until translucent, about 3 minutes, then add 4 teaspoons all-purpose (plain) flour. Cook, stirring often, to make a paste, or *roux*, about 2 minutes. Slowly whisk in 1 cup (8 fl oz/250 ml) heavy (double) cream or half-and-half (half cream), bring to a boil, reduce the heat to medium, and simmer, whisking occasionally, until very thick, about 2 minutes. Add the spinach, ½ teaspoon sea salt, ⅛ teaspoon freshly ground white or black pepper, and 1 tablespoon finely slivered fresh basil leaves and stir to combine. Taste and adjust the seasonings. Transfer to a warmed serving dish and serve right away.

Brussels Sprouts & Onion with Oregano

Whole round Brussels sprouts can't be satisfactorily sautéed—they would simply roll around in the pan. But if you slice them into ribbons, they quickly become another delicious option for this quick cooking technique.

Trim the bottoms of 1½ lb (750 g) Brussels sprouts and remove any yellowed or wilted outer leaves. Cut each sprout in half lengthwise through the core, then cut each half crosswise or lengthwise into ribbons about ¼ inch (6 mm) wide. Rinse the sprouts well in a bowl of cold water and drain in a colander. If the sprouts seem tough (as they can be late in the season), blanch the slivered leaves first for 1 minute in boiling salted water and drain.

Heat a large frying pan over medium heat. When hot, add 2 tablespoons olive oil and then 1 sliced small yellow onion and ⅛ teaspoon red pepper flakes. Cook, stirring occasionally, until the onion is softened and lightly browned, about 4 minutes. Add the Brussels sprouts along with the water clinging to them, ¼ teaspoon crumbled dried oregano, ½ teaspoon sea salt, and ¼ teaspoon freshly ground pepper. Raise the heat to high and sauté until the Brussels sprouts are tender, about 7 minutes. If the pan becomes dry and the leaves are still not soft, add ½ cup (4 fl oz/125 ml) chicken stock or water, reduce the heat to medium, and continue cooking, adding more stock or water if needed.

Add 1 teaspoon red wine vinegar or fresh lemon juice. Taste and adjust the seasonings. Transfer to a warmed serving dish and serve right away.

Stir-fried Sesame Eggplant

Because stir-frying is a fast technique, the absorbent flesh of eggplant has little time to soak up any oil. Stir-frying also sears the edges of the pieces, adding rich flavor and a nice color to the vegetable. Both large, dark purple globe eggplants and the slender, pale or dark purple Asian eggplants can be used for stir-frying. A garlicky sauce with hints of nutty sesame pairs well with the mild flesh.

1 Prepare the sauce
In a small bowl, whisk together the soy sauce, wine, vinegar, sugar, sesame oil, and garlic. Place the bowl near the stove so you can easily reach it.

2 Prepare the eggplant
If you are using globe eggplants, use a chef's knife to trim the stem end and the base, then cut in half lengthwise. Place the halves cut side down on the cutting board and cut each half lengthwise into slices about ¾ inch (2 cm) wide. Lay the slices flat and cut crosswise into sticks about ¾ inch thick. Put the eggplant strips in a bowl and toss with the salt. Transfer to a colander and let stand in the sink or over a bowl to release the bitter juices, about 1 hour. Turn the eggplant out onto several layers of paper towels and let drain; pat to absorb any excess moisture. (Alternatively, if you are using Asian eggplants, it is not necessary to salt them, as they are milder than globe eggplant. Just trim the stem ends and cut them on the diagonal into slices about 1 inch/2.5 cm thick.)

3 Ready your equipment and heat the wok
Preheat the oven to 200°F (95°C) and place a platter in the oven to warm. Have ready a wok, preferably about 14 inches (35 cm) in diameter, and 2 long-handled wooden spoons or spatulas. Be sure to turn on your kitchen ventilation to disperse any smoke. Place the wok over high heat. Hold your hand over the pan until you feel heat rising, then add 1½ teaspoons of the peanut oil. Carefully tilt and rotate the pan so that the oil is distributed evenly over the surface and is hot and shimmering.

4 Stir-fry the eggplant
Immediately add half of the eggplant and cook, tossing and stirring constantly with the 2 wooden spoons or spatulas, until golden on all sides, about 6 minutes. Transfer the stir-fried eggplant to a bowl, cover to keep hot, and repeat with the remaining 1½ teaspoons peanut oil and eggplant. Then, return the first batch of eggplant to the wok, toss to mix, and remove from the heat.

5 Add the sauce, adjust the seasonings, and serve
Pour the sauce over the eggplant and toss to coat thoroughly. Add the green onions and sesame seeds and toss once again. Taste and adjust the seasonings; often it's the sharpness of the vinegar that brings the other flavors into focus. Transfer the eggplant to the warmed platter and serve right away.

For the sauce

2 tablespoons soy sauce

1 teaspoon Shaoxing wine or dry sherry

1 teaspoon unseasoned rice vinegar

1 teaspoon sugar

1 tablespoon Asian sesame oil

1½ teaspoons minced garlic (page 32)

2 lb (1 kg) globe or Asian (slender) eggplant(s) (aubergines)

1 teaspoon sea salt, if using globe eggplant(s)

1 tablespoon peanut or grapeseed oil

3 tablespoons diagonally sliced green (spring) onions, white and tender green parts (page 33)

1 tablespoon sesame seeds, toasted (page 36)

MAKES 4–6 SERVINGS

CHEF'S TIP
Eggplant that has just been picked—the kind you find at farmers' markets—doesn't need to be salted. You will find a greater variety of eggplant at farmers' markets, as well. Rosita, Neon, and Purple Rain are a few examples of good varieties to try.

Roasted & Baked Vegetables

Roasting and baking, both done in the oven, are slow, dry-heat cooking methods. Roasting calls for slightly higher temperatures than baking and is ideal for dense root vegetables; their natural sweetness is heightened by the intense, steady heat. Baked vegetables, whether stuffed or thinly sliced and layered with other ingredients, have tender interiors enhanced by crisp, browned crusts.

Tomatoes Stuffed with Rice, Basil & Cheese

In this recipe, white rice absorbs the tomatoes' juices as they bake, and creamy mozzarella cheese binds the stuffing ingredients. Fresh basil, a classic partner for tomatoes, lends its summery flavor and aroma, and a crunchy topping of toasted bread crumbs adds texture.

1 Cook the rice for the filling

In a saucepan over medium-high heat, bring the water to a boil. As soon as you see large bubbles begin to form, add the rice and salt. When the water returns to a boil, reduce the heat to low; you want only small bubbles occasionally to break the surface. Cover the pan and cook until the water is absorbed and the rice is tender, 15–18 minutes. Transfer the rice to a large bowl to help it cool and use a fork to gently loosen the grains.

2 Prepare the green onions

While the rice is cooking, prepare the green onions. If you need help, turn to page 33. Using a chef's knife, trim off the root ends and tough green tops. Line up the onions and cut the white and about 1 inch (2.5 cm) of the tender green parts crosswise into thin slices. Reserve the remaining green parts for another use. Measure out 1 cup (3 oz/90 g) sliced onions.

3 Sliver the basil

If you need help slivering large leafy herbs, turn to page 36. Working in 2 batches, stack the basil leaves on top of one another. Roll the stack of leaves lengthwise into a tight cylinder. Using the chef's knife, cut the leaves crosswise, which will create thin slivers. These slivers are known as a *chiffonade*. Measure out 2 tablespoons slivered basil.

4 Chop the parsley

To find out more about chopping small leafy herbs, turn to page 34. Pluck the leaves from the parsley sprigs and discard the stems. Gather the leaves in a small pile on the cutting board. With the fingertips of one hand resting on top of the tip of the chef's knife, rock the blade up and down and back and forth over the leaves until they are uniformly chopped into coarse pieces. Measure out 2 tablespoons chopped parsley.

5 Shred the cheese

The easiest way to shred mozzarella, a medium-soft cheese, is to stand a box grater-shredder on a piece of parchment (baking) paper and run the cheese over the largest shredding holes. (Reserve the smallest holes for grating hard cheeses such as Parmigiano-Reggiano.) You should have about 1 cup shredded cheese. ❯

For the filling

2 cups (16 fl oz/500 ml) water

1 cup (7 oz/220 g) long-grain white rice

½ teaspoon sea salt

1 bunch green (spring) onions

12–16 leaves fresh basil

1 small bunch fresh flat-leaf (Italian) parsley

4 oz (125 g) mozzarella or Monterey jack cheese

¼ teaspoon freshly ground pepper

Olive oil for preparing the baking dish

4 or 6 large, ripe yet firm tomatoes, about ½ lb (250 g) each

2 slices slightly stale bread such as country wheat or sourdough

2 tablespoons unsalted butter or olive oil

MAKES 4 OR 6 SERVINGS

RECOMMENDED USES

Serve as the first course of a summer dinner, or as a side dish with grilled steak. For a vegetarian menu, pair with a wedge of frittata.

6 Mix the filling

Add the cheese, green onions, basil, parsley, and pepper to the rice and toss to combine. Taste and adjust the seasonings, adding more salt, a pinch at a time, to heighten the flavors, or more pepper, herbs, or green onions for a more herbaceous mixture.

7 Remove the tops from the tomatoes

Position a rack in the middle of the oven and preheat the oven to 375°F (190°C). Select a baking dish just large enough to hold the tomatoes snugly and lightly brush with olive oil. Using the chef's knife or a serrated knife, cut off a little less than the one-fourth of the top of each tomato to expose the cavities inside.

8 Remove the seeds, juices, and cores

Holding a tomato firmly in one hand, gently squeeze it over a bowl to dislodge the seeds and excess juices. Use your finger if needed to help ease out the seeds. Then, using a paring knife, carefully cut out and remove the core. If the flesh is dense and solid (as is the case with many heirloom tomatoes), cut the entire center of the tomato away from the walls. Repeat with the remaining tomatoes. Discard the seeds, juices, cores, and centers.

9 Stuff the tomatoes

Using a spoon, fill the tomatoes with the rice mixture, packing it lightly and mounding it a little above the top of each tomato. Each tomato should hold about ⅓ cup (2 oz/60 g) of the mixture. Resist the urge to pack the stuffing too tightly even if you have extra rice, or the stuffed tomatoes will be heavy and dense. Arrange the tomatoes in the prepared dish. If you have any extra rice mixture after filling the tomatoes, simply spread it in the bottom of the baking dish before adding the stuffed tomatoes. This extra stuffing will become crisp and browned in the oven.

CHEF'S TIP

Some tomatoes are better suited for stuffing than others. One heirloom variety, Striped Cavern, has large spaces inside, similar to a bell pepper, that are perfect for stuffing. After removing the seeds, it doesn't need to be hollowed out further. When choosing tomatoes for stuffing, look for ones that are large and sturdy and can stand firmly on their own.

10 Prepare the bread crumbs

For more details on making fresh bread crumbs, turn to page 37. Country wheat or sourdough bread are good choices because they have a strong and sturdy texture. Tear the bread into small pieces into the work bowl of a food processor fitted with the metal blade or into a blender. Pulse the food processor or blender until the bread pieces are processed into small crumbs.

11 Coat the bread crumbs with butter

In a small frying pan, melt the butter over medium heat. Add the bread crumbs and use a fork to stir them into the melted butter so that the crumbs are evenly coated. Coating the bread crumbs adds rich flavor. Divide the crumbs among the stuffed tomatoes, sprinkling them evenly on top and pressing them gently to help them adhere to the filling.

CHEF'S TIP

Store fresh tomatoes you grow or buy at room temperature. The cold of the refrigerator will dull their flavor and cause them to have a mealy texture.

12 Bake the tomatoes

Bake the tomatoes until the bread crumbs are golden brown, about 30 minutes. Let the tomatoes cool for 5–10 minutes to let the filling settle. Serve the tomatoes right away, when they are still hot, or wait for a little while and serve them while they are still warm.

Serving ideas

The mixture of rice, cheese, and basil used to stuff the tomatoes can be used to stuff other vegetables, too, including eggplants, bell peppers, and summer squashes. At the market, look for vegetables that, once hollowed out, will hold the same quantity of stuffing as the tomatoes. This ensures that they will bake in about 30 minutes. Summer is the best season to seek out colorful examples of these vegetables.

Asian eggplant (top left)
Cut Asian (slender) eggplants (aubergines) in half lengthwise. Leaving a ¼-inch (6-mm) wall, scoop out most of the flesh with a melon baller before stuffing.

Bell peppers (left)
Naturally hollow bell peppers (capsicums) are a common choice for stuffing. Add style to the peppers by halving them lengthwise and removing the seeds and ribs but leaving the stems attached.

Summer squash (above)
This squat green squash is a variety of heirloom zucchini (courgette), sometimes called globe squash. Slice off the stem ends, scoop out the insides, and reserve the tops to crown the finished vegetables.

Roasted Winter Root Vegetables with Rosemary

Here, a mix of cool-weather vegetables spend a long, hot spell in the oven. As they roast, the dry heat draws away moisture and coaxes the natural sugars forward. This is an especially attractive jumble of red, orange, and golden varieties, but other root vegetables can be substituted.

1 Prepare the onions

Position a rack in the center of the oven and preheat the oven to 425°F (220°C). Bring a saucepan three-fourths full of water to a boil. As soon as you see large bubbles begin to form, add the onions and cook for about 1 minute, then drain into a colander and rinse under running cold water to cool them quickly. This brief cooking in boiling water is called *blanching,* and it loosens the skins of the onions, making them easier to peel. Using a paring knife, carefully trim away the small root ends, but leave the bases intact so the onions don't fall apart when roasted. After trimming away the root ends, you should be able to use your fingers to slip the onions from their outer skins. Use the paring knife to peel away any stubborn skins.

2 Prepare the garlic

Slice the top ½ inch (12 mm) off the head(s) of garlic to expose the cloves, and rub off any loose outer papery skins. Be sure the garlic is still enclosed in a snug skin or it will dry out in the oven. (Alternatively, separate the individual cloves from the head(s) of garlic, leaving them in their skins. The individual cloves have less of a chance of drying out, since their tops are not cut off, and they will be easier to serve. However, roasted whole heads of garlic provide a more dramatic presentation.)

3 Prepare the carrots

Use a vegetable peeler to remove the skin from the carrots. Switch to a chef's knife and trim off the leafy tops or stem ends and the rootlike tips. Cut the carrots into pieces about 2½ inches (6 cm) long. Cut the thickest chunks lengthwise into quarters, and cut the medium chunks in half lengthwise.

4 Prepare the parsnips

Peel and trim the parsnips as you did the carrots. Cut into pieces about 2½ inches (6 cm) long, and halve or quarter the bigger chunks to create pieces the same size as the carrots. Using a paring knife, cut away the tough cores of the halved and quartered sections. ›

½ lb (250 g) red boiling onions

1 large or 2 small heads garlic

4 large carrots

2 large parsnips

3 golden beets

2 rutabagas

5 red potatoes

⅓ cup (3 fl oz/80 ml) olive oil

1 teaspoon sea salt

¼ teaspoon freshly ground pepper

4 sprigs fresh rosemary, each about 3 inches (7.5 cm) long

1 cup (8 fl oz/250 ml) water

6–8 sprigs fresh flat-leaf (Italian) parsley

MAKES 4–6 SERVINGS

CHEF'S TIP
Roasted vegetables are an ideal accompaniment for roasted poultry or any roasted meat, especially if you are already heating up your oven. Just roast them in a separate pan alongside or arrange the vegetables around the bird or meat in the roasting pan. If the meat finishes cooking before the vegetables, let them continue to roast while the meat is resting.

5 Prepare the beets

With a little practice, using a paring knife to peel round vegetables such as beets and rutabagas goes quickly and yields vegetables with distinct, pleasing shapes since the knife creates angled edges. (A vegetable peeler, on the other hand, is the best tool for peeling vegetables such as carrots and parsnips, whose shape will not be affected by removing their skins.) If you need help working with round vegetables, turn to page 42. Golden beets are a good choice for roasting along with other vegetables because they don't "bleed," that is, release their colored juices, the way red beets do. Use the chef's knife to trim off the stem and root ends of the beets. Then, using the paring knife and following the contour of the vegetable, cut away the thick peel. Cut the beets into wedges about the same size as the largest carrot pieces.

6 Prepare the rutabagas

Using the chef's knife, trim the top and bottom ends from the rutabagas. Using the paring knife, carefully cut away the thick peels, as you did with the beets. Switch back to the chef's knife and cut the rutabagas into wedges about the same size as the largest carrot pieces. Rutabagas will begin to discolor when exposed to the air, so prepare the other root vegetables first to minimize the rutabagas' exposure.

7 Prepare the potatoes

Using a vegetable brush, scrub the potatoes well under running cold water. Then, using the chef's knife, cut them into chunks the same size as the other vegetables. You can leave the thin skins on the red potatoes; they are nutritious and add color. Like rutabagas, potatoes will begin to discolor after cutting them; prepare them after the other root vegetables to minimize their exposure.

8 Season the vegetables

Put all the vegetables and the garlic head(s) or cloves in a large bowl. Add the olive oil, salt, and pepper and toss with your hands to coat the vegetables thoroughly with the oil. If roasting the head(s) of garlic whole, make especially sure that the cut surface is well coated to prevent the garlic from burning. Arrange the vegetables in a single layer in a large, heavy-duty roasting pan. Tuck 2 of the rosemary sprigs among the vegetables.

9 Add the water

Pour the water into the pan. Adding a little water to the roasting pan is not typical in roasting. It is included in this recipe because these dense root vegetables need the added moisture to ensure that they do not dry out too much in the initial stage of roasting.

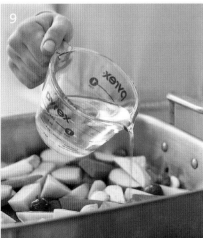

10 Roast the vegetables
Place the vegetables in the oven to begin roasting and place a serving platter on the stove top to warm from the heat of the oven. Wearing long oven mitts and using a long-handled wooden spoon or silicone spatula, stir the vegetables every 20 minutes or so during roasting to help them cook evenly. Continue roasting until the vegetables are golden brown and the biggest pieces are tender when pierced with the tip of a paring knife. Depending on the size of the pan you've used and the age and cut size of the vegetables, this will take 1–1½ hours.

11 Chop the parsley
While the vegetables are roasting, chop the parsley. If you need help chopping small leafy herbs, turn to page 34. Pluck the leaves from the parsley sprigs and discard the stems. Gather the leaves in a small pile on the cutting board. With the fingertips of one hand resting on top of the tip of the chef's knife, rock the blade up and down and back and forth over the leaves until they are uniformly chopped into coarse pieces. Measure out 4 teaspoons chopped parsley and transfer to a small bowl.

12 Mince the rosemary
For more details on mincing rosemary, turn to page 35. Carefully run your thumb and index finger down the stems of the remaining 2 rosemary sprigs to remove the leaves and discard the stems. Gather the leaves into a small pile on the cutting board and rock the blade over the leaves, as you did the parsley. Continue until the rosemary is uniformly chopped into very fine pieces, or *minced*. Measure out 2 teaspoons minced rosemary. (You have to chop the rosemary more finely than the parsley because rosemary is a much stronger-tasting herb; mincing it keeps it from overpowering a single bite. Also, the needles of rosemary can be sharp and tough if not minced.) Add the minced rosemary to the bowl with the parsley and stir to mix well.

13 Serve the vegetables
When the vegetables are done, transfer them to the warmed platter. If you roasted the head(s) of garlic whole, set them upright among the vegetables. Part of the fun of roasted garlic is squeezing out the individual cloves with your fingers (or a fork if need be). Diners can do this with the individual cloves at the table or can pull off cloves from the whole head(s) for squeezing. Taste the vegetables and evaluate the seasonings. If you feel it's needed, add a little more salt, which will heighten the natural flavors of the vegetables. Sprinkle the roasted vegetables with the parsley and rosemary and serve right away.

Serving ideas

Use the technique for roasting the assortment of root vegetables on pages 113–16 to roast other combinations of the same or similar vegetables, either on their own or in pairs. Here are three suggestions: a colorful array of beets, potatoes flavored with garlic, and carrots and parsnips left whole for visual interest. Or, create your own assortment: use about 8 cups (4 lb/2 kg) of any of the vegetables you prepared in the previous recipe.

Mixed beets (top left)

Try a mix of colors, including striped Chiogga beets. With colored beets, be sure to line your cutting board with plastic wrap to prevent stains, and separate them with aluminum foil during roasting.

Potatoes and garlic (left)

Potatoes and garlic always go well together. The red and brown fingerling potatoes shown here have a moist texture and are visually appealing.

Carrots and parsnips (above)

Carrots and parsnips are closely related, and they make a good match when roasted together. Seek out slender carrots and leave a bit of the greens attached, and cut the parsnips into long pieces.

Roasted Vegetable Variations

In Roasted Winter Root Vegetables with Rosemary (page 113), you learned the secrets—a hot oven, cutting the vegetables into the same-sized pieces for even cooking, matching the vegetables with complementary seasonings—of how to roast a colorful assortment of vegetables to create a delicious side dish. Those same secrets can be applied to a broad range of seasonal vegetables. In these variations, you'll find that this high-heat technique can be used not only for sturdy vegetables, such as potatoes, carrots, and winter squashes, but also for the more delicate ones of spring, summer, and autumn, including asparagus, tomatoes, and artichokes. Each variation makes 4 to 6 servings.

Roasted Whole Carrots with Shallots & Herbs

Shallots and herbs balance the sweetness of carrots that emerges during roasting.

Position a rack in the middle of the oven and preheat the oven to 450°F (230°C).

Peel 12 carrots about 8 inches (20 cm) long and 1 inch (2.5 cm) wide at the top, and trim off the tops. Put them in a roasting pan large enough to hold them in a single layer without crowding. Add 1 tablespoon olive oil, ½ teaspoon sea salt, and ⅛ teaspoon crumbled dried thyme. Roll the carrots in the mixture to coat them evenly, then pour in ½ cup (4 fl oz/ 125 ml) dry white wine or water.

Roast the carrots, turning them every 15 minutes, until they are a rich caramel brown in places, 40–50 minutes.

In a small frying pan over medium-low heat, melt 2 tablespoons unsalted butter. Add ¼ cup (1 oz/30 g) finely diced shallots, ¼ cup (⅓ oz/10 g) finely chopped fresh flat-leaf (Italian) parsley, 1 teaspoon minced fresh thyme, and ⅛ teaspoon freshly ground pepper. Cook, stirring, until the shallots are fragrant, 1–2 minutes. Spoon over the carrots and turn to coat evenly. Transfer to a warmed platter and serve right away.

Roasted Baby Artichokes

Roasting over high heat brings out the nutty essence of artichokes.

Position a rack in the middle of the oven and preheat the oven to 400°F (200°C). Zest and juice 2 lemons. Set aside the zest and add the juice to a bowl of cold water.

Have ready 20–24 baby artichokes. Working with 1 artichoke at a time, snap off the outer leaves until you reach the pale inner leaves. Using a serrated knife, cut off the top one-third, then trim the base and stems with a paring knife. Halve the artichoke lengthwise and transfer to the lemon water.

Drain the artichokes and transfer to a large, dry bowl. Toss with 3 tablespoons olive oil, ¾ teaspoon sea salt, and ¼ teaspoon freshly ground pepper, then arrange in a roasting pan. Add 1 bay leaf and 1 sprig fresh thyme and pour in ½ cup (4 fl oz/125 ml) dry white wine or water.

Roast the artichokes, stirring them every 15 minutes, until tender, 35–45 minutes.

In a small bowl, combine the lemon zest, 1 finely diced shallot, and 1 tablespoon finely chopped fresh tarragon. Toss with the artichokes, transfer to a warmed serving dish, and serve right away.

Roasted Cherry Tomatoes

Small cherry tomatoes fast-roasted at a high temperature come out of the oven sweet and molten. They burst and release their juices, delicious in succulent bites or crushed into a sauce to spoon over fish or grilled polenta.

Position a rack in the middle of the oven and preheat the oven to 425°F (220°C).

Rinse 1½–2 pints (18–24 oz/560–750 g) small cherry tomatoes such as grape, yellow pear, or other fruit-named varieties. Pinch off the stems if desired. Put the tomatoes in a baking dish large enough to hold them in a single layer and toss with 4 teaspoons olive oil and ¼ teaspoon sea salt.

Roast until the skins begin to split and release some juices into the hot dish, 5–7 minutes, depending on the size of the tomatoes. Add ⅛ teaspoon freshly ground pepper and toss well. Taste and adjust the seasonings. Transfer to a warmed serving dish and serve right away.

Roasted Delicata Squash with Spicy Red Butter

Seasoned with paprika, cumin, and other spices and fresh herbs, this spicy red butter balances the earthy, sweet flavor of winter squash.

Position a rack in the middle of the oven and preheat the oven to 375°F (190°C). Select a roasting pan large enough to hold the squash halves in a single layer without crowding and lightly coat with olive oil.

Cut 4–6 delicata squashes, about ½ lb (250 g) each, in half through the stem end. Scoop out the seeds and discard them. Brush each half with ½ teaspoon olive oil and rub a pinch of sea salt into the flesh of each. Arrange the halves, cut side down, in the prepared pan. Pour in ¼ cup (2 fl oz/60 ml) water. Roast until tender when pierced with the tip of a paring knife, 25–30 minutes.

Meanwhile, in a bowl, combine 4 tablespoons (2 oz/60 g) room-temperature unsalted butter, 1 minced green (spring) onion (white and tender green parts), 1 tablespoon fresh lime juice, and 2 teaspoons *each* chopped fresh flat-leaf (Italian) parsley and cilantro (fresh coriander). Stir to distribute the herbs, then add 2 teaspoons paprika, 1 teaspoon ground cumin, ¼ teaspoon ground coriander, ¼ teaspoon sea salt, and ⅛ teaspoon cayenne pepper. Stir to mix well. Taste and adjust the seasonings.

When the squash is done, arrange the halves, cut side up, on a warmed platter or individual plates and place a dollop of the spicy butter in each cavity. Serve right away.

Roasted Potato Wedges

Moist, low-starch potatoes such as white potatoes, creamers, and fingerlings, or medium-starch varieties such as Yukon gold are excellent candidates for roasting.

Position a rack in the middle of the oven and preheat the oven to 400°F (200°C).

Select 2 lb (1 kg) low- or medium-starch potatoes that are more or less the same size. Scrub them well but do not peel. Cut the potatoes lengthwise into 2-inch (5-cm) wedges. (Alternatively, you can use small varieties such as new potatoes or new fingerlings. Leave them whole or cut into halves or quarters.) Arrange the potatoes in a roasting pan large enough to hold them in a single layer.

In a small frying pan over medium heat, melt 6 tablespoons (3 oz/90 g) unsalted butter. Reduce the heat to medium-low and cook for 1 minute to evaporate the excess water in the butter. Remove from the heat and let stand for 2 minutes. Using a metal spoon, skim the foam from the surface of the butter and discard it. Pour the butter through a fine-mesh sieve over the potatoes.

Add ½ teaspoon sea salt and toss the potatoes to coat evenly with the butter. Roast the potatoes, turning them every 12 minutes or so, until golden and tender when pierced with the tip of a paring knife, about 25 minutes. Taste and adjust the seasonings with salt or freshly ground pepper, if desired.

Transfer to a warmed serving dish and serve right away.

Roasted Sweet Potatoes with Soy Glaze

Here, sweet potatoes are roasted whole to conserve their moisture, then they are split, brushed with a sweet-salty soy glaze, and again roasted briefly.

Position a rack in the middle of the oven and preheat the oven to 400°F (200°C).

Scrub 4 orange-fleshed sweet potatoes, such as Garnet, Jewel, or Beauregard, about ½ lb (250 g) each. Put them on a rimmed baking sheet and prick each in a few places with a fork. Bake until tender when pierced with the tip of a paring knife, 50–60 minutes.

In a small saucepan over medium-high heat, combine ¼ cup (2 fl oz/60 ml) *each* mirin and fresh orange juice, 2 tablespoons soy sauce, 2 tablespoons firmly packed brown sugar, and 1 tablespoon unsalted butter and bring to a boil, stirring to melt the butter. Let the mixture cook until large, thick bubbles form on the surface and it has reduced to ¼–⅓ cup (2–3 fl oz/60–80 ml), about 5 minutes.

When the sweet potatoes are done, transfer them to a cutting board. Leave the oven on. Holding them steady with tongs, slice each potato in half lengthwise. Use the tip of a paring knife to score a crisscross pattern on the cut surface of each half.

Arrange the potato halves, cut side up, in a lightly buttered baking dish large enough to hold them in a single layer without crowding. Brush the scored surface with the glaze and return to the oven. Bake until the glaze seeps into the flesh and the tops are glossy in places, 5–7 minutes longer. Serve right away.

Summer Squash Tian

A tian is a Provençal preparation in which vegetables are slowly baked until meltingly tender. Here, the true flavor of green and yellow squashes emerges when the beautiful ovals are baked over a bed of softened, herb-flecked onions. A drizzle of fruity olive oil just before serving adds a final touch of flavor.

1 Prepare the onions

If you are not sure how to dice an onion, turn to page 30. Using a chef's knife, cut the onions in half lengthwise and peel each half. One at a time, place the onion halves, cut side down, on a cutting board. Make a series of parallel vertical cuts, being sure to stop just short of the root end (this holds the onion half together as you cut). Then make a series of parallel horizontal cuts and finally crosswise cuts to create ½-inch (12-mm) dice.

2 Prepare the herbs

To find out more about chopping small branched herbs, turn to page 35. First, chop the marjoram: Gently run your thumb and index finger down the marjoram sprigs to remove the leaves and then discard the stems. Gather the leaves in a small pile on the cutting board. With the fingertips of one hand resting on top of the tip of the chef's knife, rock the blade up and down and back and forth over the leaves until they are uniformly chopped into coarse pieces. Measure out 2 tablespoons chopped marjoram. Repeat to strip and chop the thyme leaves and measure out 1 teaspoon. Set the herbs aside separately.

3 Mince the garlic

For more details on working with garlic, turn to page 32. Place the clove on a cutting board, firmly press against it with the flat side of the chef's knife, and pull away the papery skin. Cut the clove in half lengthwise, then thinly slice the halves lengthwise. Rock the blade of the knife over the garlic slices until coarsely chopped. Clean off any bits of garlic from the knife, gather the pieces into a compact pile, and continue to chop until the garlic pieces are evenly chopped into very fine pieces, or *minced.* ›

2 red onions, about 1 lb (500 g) total weight

1 small bunch fresh marjoram or oregano

2 or 3 sprigs fresh thyme

1 small clove garlic

1 lb (500 g) green zucchini (courgettes)

1 lb (500 g) yellow zucchini (courgettes), such as Gold Bar, or young crookneck squash

3 tablespoons olive oil, plus extra for preparing the dish, brushing on top, and drizzling over the *tian*

⅓ cup (3 fl oz/80 ml) dry white wine, chicken stock, or canned low-sodium chicken broth

¾ teaspoon sea salt

¼ teaspoon freshly ground pepper

MAKES 4–6 SERVINGS

4 Prepare the squash

Rinse the squash under running cold water and dry thoroughly. Trim the stem ends and discard. Using the chef's knife, cut each squash crosswise on the diagonal into slices about ¼ inch (6 mm) thick. Cutting on the diagonal yields particularly attractive slices that are also easier to layer in the *tian* than if you cut them into straight rounds. Discard the round blossom ends.

5 Cook the onions

Position a rack in the middle of the oven and preheat the oven to 350°F (180°C). Lightly oil a shallow 2-qt (2-l) baking dish. Heat a large frying pan over medium-high heat. When hot, add 2 tablespoons of the olive oil and let it heat for several seconds. When the surface of the oil appears to shimmer, it is sufficiently hot. Add the onions and stir with a wooden spoon to coat them evenly with the oil. Cook, stirring often, until the onions are fragrant and lightly browned on the edges, about 5 minutes.

6 Season the onions and add the wine

Add the marjoram, half of the thyme, and the garlic to the pan with the onions and stir to combine. Add the wine and simmer until it has evaporated, about 2 minutes (the flavor will remain in the pan). Stir in ½ teaspoon of the salt and ⅛ teaspoon of the pepper. Scoop the onions into the prepared dish and spread them out evenly with the back of the spoon. >

CHEF'S TIP

For a tian with a handsome, uniform appearance, stick to zucchini or young crookneck squash for this recipe; these tend to be more or less the same in diameter from end to end and therefore create slices of about the same size. Large, bulbous crookneck squash would yield ovals of different sizes.

7 Assemble the *tian*

Layer the squash over the onions in the dish, overlapping the slices and alternating the colors as you go. The number of layers will depend on the size of the dish and the size of the squash. Be sure to use all of the squash slices, even if it feels as if you're crowding them or they are rising too high in the dish; they will shrink considerably as they bake. Sprinkle the top with the remaining ½ teaspoon thyme, ¼ teaspoon salt, and ⅛ teaspoon pepper.

8 Partially bake the *tian*

Cover the assembled *tian* with aluminum foil and bake for about 30 minutes. Covering the *tian* with foil will allow the squash to cook without drying out too much during the initial stages of baking.

CHEF'S TIP

A tian provides a great format for improvisation. Along with the squash used here, you could include sliced eggplant or plum (Roma) tomatoes or thinly sliced potatoes. Or, when sautéing the onions in step 5, add a bit of chopped bell pepper (capsicum) or tomato.

9 Brush the *tian* with oil

Remove the *tian* from the oven and remove the foil. Using a pastry brush, brush the remaining 1 tablespoon olive oil over the top layer of squash. This will keep the slices from drying out as they continue to bake and it will add a little flavor. Return the *tian* to the oven and bake until the squash slices are tender when pierced with the tip of a paring knife and lightly browned, about 1 hour longer.

10 Serve the *tian*

Let the *tian* cool on a wire rack for 10–15 minutes before serving to allow the contents to settle. This is a rustic dish, so it's fine to use a wide metal spoon or spatula to scoop it out for serving (you don't need to cut it into neat squares). Drizzle each serving with olive oil and serve hot, warm, or at room temperature.

Finishing touches

Baked vegetable dishes don't need to be assembled in a single large dish. You can layer the squash slices and onions in individual baking dishes—an easy idea well suited for entertaining. A final drizzle of olive oil dresses up this rustic tian, *but you can add other Provençal-inspired garnishes with the oil, such as fresh goat cheese and basil. Or, top the finished* tian *with bread crumbs toasted in butter for flavor and texture.*

Topped with goat cheese and basil (top left)
After drizzling each serving with olive oil, top with a scattering of tangy crumbled fresh goat cheese and small fresh basil leaves.

Baked in individual dishes (left)
Layer the cooked onions and squash in six 1-cup (8–fl oz/250 ml) baking dishes. Start with the onions and end with the squash for a total of 4 layers. Cover with aluminum foil and bake for 30 minutes. Uncover, brush with oil, and bake for 30–40 minutes longer.

Sprinkled with toasted bread crumbs (above)
Melt 2 tablespoons unsalted butter in a frying pan over low heat. Add ⅔ cup (1⅓ oz/40 g) fresh bread crumbs and toast, stirring frequently, about 5 minutes.

Classic Potato Gratin

The secret to the success of a delectable gratin lies in slicing the potatoes very thinly so that they adhere to one another in tender layers when baked. A mandoline—a flat, rectangular cutting tool—is ideal for quickly cutting the potatoes into thin, uniform slices. Here, pungent Gruyère cheese contributes to the definitive browned crust.

1 clove garlic

2 cups (16 fl oz/500 ml) half-and-half (half cream) or a mixture of equal parts whole milk and heavy (double) cream

Unsalted butter for preparing the dish

2½ lb (1.25 kg) potatoes, preferably Yukon gold

5 oz (155 g) Gruyère cheese

1 teaspoon sea salt

½ teaspoon freshly ground pepper

MAKES 4–6 SERVINGS

CHEF'S TIP

Serving a rich square of potato gratin atop a bed of greens is a simple idea for an appealing presentation. Simply toss a mix of young spring greens with your favorite vinaigrette.

1 Prepare the garlic

Place the garlic clove on a cutting board and press against it firmly with the flat side of a chef's knife until the papery skin splits and the clove is smashed but still intact. Peel away the skin. Smashing but not chopping the garlic lets you use it to flavor the half-and-half and then more easily remove it later.

2 Steep the garlic in the half-and-half

In a small saucepan, combine the garlic and half-and-half. Place the pan over medium-low heat and heat just until tiny bubbles appear around the edge of the pan, about 5 minutes. Heating the mixture helps transfer the aromatic flavor of the garlic to the half-and-half. Don't let the half-and-half come to a boil; this causes a skin to form and will affect the texture. Remove the saucepan from the heat, cover, and let stand to infuse the half-and-half with the flavor of the garlic. After 10 minutes, remove the garlic with a slotted spoon and discard it. Re-cover the pan to keep the half-and-half warm.

3 Peel the potatoes

While the garlic is steeping in the half-and-half, position a rack in the middle of the oven and preheat the oven to 375°F (190°C). Butter a 9-by-12-inch (23-by-30-cm) baking dish. Using a paring knife, peel the potatoes. If you need help working with round vegetables, turn to page 42. Have ready a bowl three-fourths full of cold water. Working with 1 potato at a time, cut off the ends. Following the contour of the potato, cut away skins using quick, long strokes down the length of the potato. (Peeling the potatoes with a knife will give them a nicer, more distinct shape with angular edges. Alternatively, you could use a vegetable peeler.) Transfer the peeled potato to the bowl and immerse in the water and repeat with the remaining potatoes. Keeping the peeled potatoes submerged in water will prevent them from discoloring.

4 Cut the potatoes into thin slices

Again working with 1 potato at a time, remove a peeled potato from the water and pat dry. Using a mandoline or mandoline-style kitchen slicer, slice the potatoes into rounds about ⅛ inch (3 mm) thick. Transfer the slices to a separate bowl without any water so the slices don't lose their starch; the starch helps bind the gratin together. (Alternatively, cut the potatoes into slices ⅛ inch thick using a sharp chef's knife, being careful to make the slices as uniform as you can.) >

5 Shred the cheese

The easiest way to shred Gruyère, a medium-soft cheese, is to stand a box grater-shredded on a piece of parchment (baking) paper and run the cheese over the largest shredding holes. (Reserve the smallest holes for grating hard cheeses such as Parmigiano-Reggiano.) You should have about 1¼ cups shredded cheese.

6 Assemble the gratin

Put roughly one-fourth of the potato slices in the prepared dish and spread them in an even layer. Sprinkle with ¼ teaspoon of the salt, ⅛ teaspoon freshly ground pepper, and one-fourth of the shredded cheese. Repeat this layering 3 more times for a total of 4 layers. When assembling the last layer of potatoes, take a moment to overlap them neatly and attractively before sprinkling with the salt, pepper, and cheese. This will lend a finished look to the baked gratin.

7 Add the half-and-half

Pour the warm half-and-half over the potatoes. The potatoes will absorb the liquid as they bake.

8 Bake the gratin

Bake until the surface of the gratin is golden brown on top and the potatoes are tender when pierced with the tip of a paring knife, about 35 minutes. Let the gratin rest on a wire rack for 10 minutes to allow it to settle, then use a chef's knife to cut it into squares. Remove the squares with a spatula and serve right away.

> **MAKE-AHEAD TIP**
> *To make the gratin ahead of time, follow the recipe as written, but remove the gratin from the oven just before the potatoes are fully tender, after 25–30 minutes. Let stand at room temperature for up to 2 hours. Cover the cooled, partially baked gratin with aluminum foil and finish baking in a preheated 350°F (180°C) until heated through, about 25 minutes.*

Gratin Variations

Classic Potato Gratin (page 126) shows how a starchy vegetable can slowly absorb a seasoned liquid, turning the vegetable soft, succulent, and golden in the process. This basic method can be applied to other vegetables as well, as these variations illustrate. First, starchy sweet potatoes, which are briefly boiled to soften them, drink up a chipotle-flavored cream. Then, nonstarchy fennel and leeks rely on the starch of Irish potatoes to bind them together. Finally, dense winter squash and a good melting cheese are layered with sweet caramelized onions. These hearty dishes are versatile as well, performing equally well as main courses or side dishes. Each variation makes 4 to 6 servings.

Sweet Potato Gratin

Smoky, spicy chipotle chiles and mellow cream temper the sweetness of these aptly named tubers.

Position a rack in the middle of the oven and preheat the oven to 375°F (190°C). Bring a large saucepan three-fourths full of water to a boil.

In a separate saucepan, combine 1 cup (8 fl oz/250 ml) chicken stock, 1 cup (8 fl oz/250 ml) heavy (double) cream, and 1 tablespoon puréed chipotle chile in adobo sauce and bring just to a boil over medium heat. Remove from the heat and taste, adding more chipotle purée if desired. Set aside, cover, and keep warm.

Peel 2½ lb (1.25 kg) orange-fleshed sweet potatoes and cut into slices ⅛ inch (3 mm) thick. Add 1 tablespoon sea salt and the potato slices to the boiling water. Cook until partially softened, about 3 minutes, and drain.

Spread one-fourth of the potato slices in a buttered 9-by-12-inch (23-by-30-cm) baking dish. Sprinkle with ¼ teaspoon sea salt. Repeat this layering 3 times. Pour the cream mixture over the potatoes, cover with aluminum foil, and bake for 25 minutes. Uncover and continue baking until the potatoes are tender, about 20 minutes longer.

Fennel & Potato Gratin

Fennel mixed with high-starch potatoes makes a satisfying gratin.

Position a rack in the middle of the oven and preheat the oven to 350°F (180°C).

Cut 2 lb (1 kg) trimmed fennel bulbs in half from top to bottom, going right through the core. Cut out the cores and cut the halves lengthwise or crosswise into slices ¼ inch (6 mm) thick.

In a large frying pan over medium heat, melt 2 tablespoons unsalted butter. Add the fennel and cook, stirring often, until partially softened, about 5 minutes. Add 1 cup (3 oz/90 g) thinly sliced leeks and continue cooking to heat through, about 1 minute longer. Transfer to a large bowl.

Peel 1¼ lb (625 g) russet potatoes and cut into slices ⅛ inch (3 mm) thick. Add the slices to the fennel mixture along with 1 teaspoon sea salt and ¼ teaspoon freshly ground white pepper. Toss to mix thoroughly, then stir in 1 cup (8 fl oz/250 ml) each chicken stock and heavy (double) cream. Transfer the mixture to a buttered 9-by-12-inch (23-by-30-cm) baking dish and spread evenly. Bake until the vegetables are tender, about 1 hour.

Butternut Squash Gratin

The flavorful flesh of butternut squash has the perfect density for a gratin.

Position a rack in the middle of the oven and preheat the oven to 375°F (190°C).

Cut 2 yellow onions into slices ½ inch (12 mm) thick. In a large frying pan over high heat, warm 1 tablespoon each unsalted butter and olive oil. Add the onions and 1 tablespoon chopped fresh sage leaves and cook for 5 minutes. Reduce the heat to medium-low, cover, and cook, stirring once or twice, until the onions are soft, about 20 minutes. Stir in ½ teaspoon sea salt and ⅛ teaspoon freshly ground pepper.

Peel the 8-inch (20-cm) neck of 1 butternut squash. Cut the neck in half lengthwise, then into ¼-inch (6-mm) half-rounds. Steam for 5 minutes (see page 57). Transfer half of the squash to a buttered 9-by-12-inch (23-by-30-cm) baking dish and sprinkle with ⅛ teaspoon each sea salt and pepper and ⅓ cup (1½ oz/45 g) shredded Gruyère cheese. Top with the onions, then add ⅓ cup cheese and the remaining squash. Sprinkle with ⅓ cup cheese, pour 1 cup (8 fl oz/250 ml) warm heavy (double) cream over the top, and sprinkle with ½ cup (1 oz/30 g) fresh bread crumbs. Bake about 30 minutes.

Roasted Asparagus with Orange-Shallot Butter

Asparagus, a treasured spring vegetable, benefits from roasting in a hot oven, which intensifies its flavor and gives it a slightly smoky taste. In this recipe, the tender, dark green spears are cloaked with a simple but rich butter sauce that combines sweet orange juice and mildly pungent shallots.

1 Trim the asparagus
If you are using thick asparagus, use a chef's knife to cut away the bottom of each spear where it starts to change color, becoming paler and visibly tougher. Discard the ends. Using a vegetable peeler, peel the outer green skin from each thick spear to within about 2 inches (5 cm) of the tip. (Alternatively, if you are using thin asparagus—about the width of a pencil—lightly hold a spear with your fingers and begin bending it at the end opposite the tip until it breaks naturally; the spear will snap precisely where the fibrous, tough, paler inedible portion begins. Discard the ends. You don't need to peel thin spears.)

2 Season the asparagus
Position a rack in the middle of the oven and preheat the oven to 425°F (220°C). Place a serving platter on the stove top to warm from the heat of the oven. Put the asparagus in a baking dish large enough to hold the spears in a single layer. Add the olive oil and salt and toss to coat well.

3 Roast the asparagus
Put the asparagus into the oven and roast, turning them one or twice, until the spears are shriveled a bit and tender when pierced with the tip of a paring knife, 15–25 minutes, depending on their thickness.

4 Make the butter sauce
To find out more about juicing citrus, turn to page 38. Cut the orange in half crosswise and, using a handheld reamer or a citrus juicer, squeeze out the juice. In a small saucepan over medium-high heat, combine the orange juice and shallots and bring to a boil. Reduce the heat until only small bubbles occasionally break the surface, and simmer until the juice has reduced to 1½ tablespoons, 4–5 minutes. Remove from the heat, add the butter pieces a few at a time, and whisk until melted. Season with a pinch of salt and the pepper.

5 Serve the asparagus
Transfer the asparagus to the warmed platter, pour the butter over the top, and serve right away.

1½ lb (750 g) thick or thin asparagus spears

2 teaspoons olive oil

½ teaspoon sea salt, plus extra for seasoning the butter

1 orange

2 shallots, finely diced (page 31)

3 tablespoons cold unsalted butter, cut into small pieces

⅛ teaspoon freshly ground pepper

MAKES 4–6 SERVINGS

CHEF'S TIP
The juice of a blood orange, with its intense purple color and berrylike flavor, can be used in the sauce. The sweet juice of Meyer lemons is another delicious option.

Using Key Tools & Equipment

A kitchen stocked with the basics—a carefully chosen selection of pots and pans, a set of sharp knives, an array of frequently used tools such as a swivel-bladed vegetable peeler and a sturdy box grater-shredder—is the key to all kinds of cooking, from boiling pasta and braising meats to sautéing fish and roasting poultry. Fortunately, this same equipment will serve you well for cooking a wide variety of vegetables.

Steaming & Boiling

For boiling vegetables, you'll need a large pot. An 8-quart (8-l) stockpot, which allows plenty of room for the boiling water to move around sizable vegetables, is a good choice. A large saucepan is fine for smaller vegetables, such as green beans or chunks of potato.

You'll also need a good-sized saucepan with a tight-fitting lid for steaming. When the saucepan is paired with a collapsible steamer basket and a little boiling water, you have the perfect set-up for steaming vegetables. When opened, the wide elevated basket lets steam from the water surround the vegetables in an enclosed environment and cook them gently.

Special steamer inserts that rest inside the top of a saucepan are available as well. They are ideal for steaming dense vegetables because they allow you to use a larger amount of water and free you from having to check the level as often.

Braising

The best pan for braising vegetables (which don't need to be cooked as long as stews or large cuts of meat) is actually a sauté pan. These pans are wide and have straight sides higher than a frying pan but lower than a saucepan. A sauté pan about 10 inches (25 cm) in diameter with 3-inch (7.5-cm) sides is the most practical size.

An important feature of any pan that you use for braising is a tight-fitting lid. The lid prevents the moderate amount of braising liquid from evaporating, ensuring that the vegetables cook slowly in the simmering liquid. Covering the pan also preserves some of the liquid, so you can use it to make a sauce.

There are also special pans specifically designed for braising called braisers. They have a domed lid that allows moisture to drip back down into the pan, and two short handles that make the pan easy to lift and transfer. When braising bulky vegetables, such as sliced cabbage, an enameled cast-iron Dutch oven works well because its sides are higher than the sides of a sauté pan. Whichever pan you use, make sure that it's made from a heavy nonreactive material so that it will conduct heat evenly and won't react with such acidic ingredients as tomatoes, wine, vinegar, or citrus juices.

Sautéing & Stir-frying

When it comes to sautéing vegetables, the pan of choice for beginners is a frying pan, rather than a sauté pan. The sloped sides of a frying pan (sometimes called a skillet) make it easier to toss small pieces of vegetables in the pan, which prevents them from sticking and browning too much. Tossing also helps them absorb heat at a faster rate.

Frying pans come in a variety of sizes and most kitchens should have both a smaller one, about 10 inches (25 cm), and a larger 12- or 14-inch (30- to 35-cm) pan. Nonreactive pans, either made of or lined with stainless steel so they won't react with acidic ingredients, are a good everyday choice. Old-fashioned cast-iron pans work well for roasting dense potatoes and can easily move from the stove top to the oven. Make sure they are enameled, or they will react with acidic ingredients.

A thin metal wok is the best tool for stir-frying because it heats quickly, exposing the food to an evenly hot surface. The flared sides of a wok maximize the cooking area and keep the ingredients from spilling out of the pan as you stir.

If you don't have a wok, a large frying pan is a good substitute.

Roasting & Baking

For roasting root vegetables, you'll need a roasting pan, preferably one that is thick and heavy so that it conducts heat evenly and well. You'll also want the pan to be large enough so that the vegetables are not crowded; vegetables with too little space will not develop rich brown exteriors. It's fine to use a heavy-duty rimmed baking sheet for baking potatoes.

When baking vegetables, ceramic or tempered glass baking dishes are a good choice because they hold heat well and are attractive enough to bring to the table. The dishes come in all sizes, including individual ones. Setting a pan or dish of roasted or baked vegetables on a wire rack after they have finished cooking will facilitate cooling.

Knives & Cutting Boards

You'll use a knife to prepare almost all the vegetables you cook, so having good, sharp knives is essential. A paring knife will efficiently peel round vegetables, test vegetables for doneness, or mince small items such as shallots. You'll need a chef's knife for slicing, chopping, and mincing. A serrated knife comes in handy for slicing tough artichokes or delicate-skinned vegetables such as ripe tomatoes.

It's best to reserve one cutting board in your kitchen just for preparing vegetables. Keep a separate board for raw meat and poultry to prevent bacteria from spreading, and yet another board for fruits to avoid compromising their sweet flavors.

Peelers & Slicers

A vegetable peeler is an indispensable tool. You will rely on it for quickly peeling carrots, asparagus, and other vegetables with shapes not affected by peeling. Seek out one with a swivel blade, which will hug the curves of a vegetable for easy maneuverability.

To reduce the amount of time needed to slice vegetables thinly, such as potatoes for a gratin, invest in a mandoline or a mandoline-style kitchen slicer.

Shredders, Graters & Juicers

A box grater-shredder has holes for shredding (larger, teardrop-shaped holes) and grating (small rasps). A fine rasp grater, such as a Microplane grater, does double duty: it quickly grates hard cheeses and removes the colored zest from citrus. A handheld citrus reamer, a rounded, ridged tool with a sharp point, easily extracts the juice from citrus halves of all sizes.

Mixing Bowls

It's a good idea to have a set of tempered glass or stainless-steel bowls for everyday use. The smaller ones can hold prepped ingredients for your *mise en place,* while the largest bowls are ideal for tossing vegetables with oil and other seasonings.

Measuring Tools

To ensure correct volume, have on hand both dry and liquid measuring cups and a set of measuring spoons.

Processors & Grinders

There are numerous tools to help you grind ingredients. A food processor quickly grinds stale bread into crumbs. A small electric coffee mill lets you grind whole spices to release their flavor; reserve it just for this use. A mortar and pestle will also grind spices and is the traditional

tool for making pesto. Finally, no kitchen is complete without a pepper mill. Freshly grinding your own pepper is essential for the best flavor.

Mashing Tools

For smooth mashed potatoes, nothing beats a ricer. Its plunger pushes cooked potatoes (or other vegetables) through a perforated metal disk, efficiently breaking them down. For chunkier mixtures, use a handheld masher, either one with holes or a series of sturdy metal bands.

Spoons, Spatulas & Skimmers

You'll use a wide assortment of spoons, spatulas, and skimmers when cooking vegetables. Wooden spoons are traditional for stirring mixtures and sauces; those with corners let you reach the edges of pans without scratching them when

deglazing. Spatulas made of silicone withstand high temperatures, making them a good choice for stirring hot mixtures. Metal spoons (either solid or slotted) and wide skimmers help you transfer cooked vegetables more easily.

Colanders, Sieves & Spinners

Use a metal colander for rinsing and draining vegetables in general. You can also use it to let the moisture drain away from salted eggplant. A fine-mesh sieve helps strain the grit from the liquid used to soak dried mushrooms. You can use a lettuce spinner for both spinning greens dry and for rinsing them (see page 40).

Kitchen Linens

Handling hot pans and serving dishes calls for a supply of thick potholders and oven mitts. You will use kitchen towels

to absorb excess moisture from vegetables, such as boiled green beans. When paired with a fine-mesh sieve, cheesecloth (muslin) helps strain soaking liquids.

Miscellaneous Tools

Use tongs to turn spears of roasted asparagus or hold hot potatoes. Kitchen scissors quickly snip chives. A sturdy brush helps clean root vegetables, and a pastry brush lets you brush vegetables with oil as they bake to prevent drying. Finally, a whisk makes quick work of mixing seasonings into liquids and stirring many sauces.

Serving Dishes

Collect an assortment of heatproof bowls and platters, which can be preheated in your oven (see page 17) and will help keep vegetables warm when served.

Glossary

ARTICHOKE This vegetable is actually the flower bud harvested from a plant of the thistle family. Baby artichokes are not immature artichokes, but simply small ones that grow lower on the plant. All artichokes have a mild, nutty flavor, should be heavy for their size, and have tightly closed leaves.

ASPARAGUS These tall, tender-crisp spears can be as thin as a pencil or as thick as your thumb, and the two thicknesses should be prepared differently (see page 89). Look for firm stalks and tight, dry tips.

BEANS, GREEN Also called snap beans, string beans, or runner beans, green beans have a mild, grassy flavor. Blue Lake, about 5 inches (13 cm) long and with a rounded pod, is a common variety. Haricots verts, a French variety, are small, slender, and dark green and have a tender texture.

BEETS This hardy root vegetable often boasts a deep, rich red color combined with a sweet, earthy flavor. Today it is not unusual to find pink, golden, white, and even striped beets. Look for firm beets with smooth skins and no bruising. Fresh beets should have the greens attached and 1 to 2 inches (2.5 to 5 cm) of the root ends.

BELGIAN ENDIVE These tightly furled shoots have been painstakingly cultivated to form small, pale, elongated heads. Belgian endive, which has a pleasantly bitter flavor, is also known as witloof or chicory.

BELL PEPPERS Also called sweet peppers and capsicums, bell peppers come in a range of colors. Green bell peppers are immature, have a sharp flavor, and do not ripen once picked. Red bell peppers are simply a more mature (and sweeter) stage of green bell peppers. Other colors are separate varieties. Look for heavy-fleshed, unwaxed peppers.

BLACK KALE Also called *cavolo nero* or Tuscan kale, this member of the cabbage family is not really black, but rather a deep, dark green. The crinkled leaves have a hearty and robust flavor and hold their texture well when cooked.

BOK CHOY, BABY Also known as Shanghai bok choy, pale green, tender baby bok choy has a flavor somewhere between celery and cabbage. Give particular attention to the base when rinsing, as grit is usually lodged between the stems.

BREAD CRUMBS, FRESH These crumbs add a textured topping to baked vegetable dishes. You can make them at home by processing stale bread (see page 37).

BROCCOLI RABE Also known as broccoli raab, rape, and rapini, broccoli rabe has a mild, pleasantly bitter taste. Despite its name, this bright green vegetable, with its many jagged leaves, slender stalks, and small florets, does not closely resemble broccoli. Before cooking, remove and discard any tough stems and wilted leaves.

BRUSSELS SPROUTS Members of the cabbage family, Brussels sprouts grow on long, curving stalks as small, tightly closed heads. Select sprouts that are heavy for their size and bright green.

BUTTERMILK Made by adding bacteria to skimmed milk to convert the sugars to acid, buttermilk is slightly thick and tangy.

BUTTER, UNSALTED Unsalted butter gives cooks more control over the seasoning of a dish. It also tends to be fresher because salt acts as a preservative, lengthening the shelf life of butter at the supermarket.

CABBAGE Cabbage leaves may be pale green or red, with green cabbage the most plentiful. Red cabbage has thicker leaves and a faintly peppery taste. Another variety, savoy, has crinkled green leaves. Buy firm, heavy heads with closely furled leaves.

CAPERS The unopened flower buds of bushes native to the Mediterranean, capers are dried, cured, and then usually packed in a vinegar brine. Rinse them before using.

CAYENNE A very hot ground red pepper made from dried cayenne and other chiles. Use cayenne pepper sparingly to add heat or heighten flavors.

CELERY ROOT Also known as celeriac, celery root is a knobby, round autumn vegetable with a taste similar to common celery but with a more pronounced nutty, earthy flavor and a softer, dense texture. Buy firm, medium-sized roots that feel heavy for their size and are free of bruising.

CHARD Often called Swiss chard, this leafy cooking green has large, crinkled leaves on fleshy, ribbed stems. There are two main varieties: one with red stems and another with pearly white stems. Rainbow chard, also commonly found, may have red, pink, or yellow stems. Chard with red stems has a slightly earthier flavor, while chard with white or yellow stems tends to be sweeter.

CHEESES
Whether sprinkled over a finished dish, mixed into a stuffing to bind it, or layered between potato slices, cheese plays an important role in many vegetable recipes. Always grate or shred cheese just before using to ensure the freshest flavor.

Fresh goat Made from goat's milk, fresh goat cheese has a mild, tangy flavor and a slightly crumbly or smooth, spreadable texture.

Gruyère This semifirm, dense, smooth cow's milk cheese is produced in Switzerland and France and is appreciated for its mild, nutty flavor and superior melting properties.

Monterey jack A soft, white cow's milk cheese that originated in California. It has a mild flavor and melts well.

Mozzarella This mild, creamy cheese made from cow's milk or water buffalo's milk is formed into balls. If possible, seek out fresh mozzarella packed in water or whey, rather than the larger vacuum-sealed cheeses.

Parmigiano-Reggiano The "true" Parmesan cheese, this is an aged, hard cheese made from partially skimmed cow's milk. It has a nutty flavor and rich fragrance and develops areas with a subtle granular texture as it ages.

Pecorino romano A pleasantly salty Italian sheep's milk cheese with a grainy texture, *pecorino romano* is primarily used for grating.

CHIPOTLE CHILES The dried and smoked form of jalapeño chiles, chipotles are often packed in an oniony tomato-vinegar mixture known as adobo sauce.

CLOVES Shaped like a small nail with a round head, the clove is the dried bud of a tropical evergreen tree. Cloves have a strong, sweet flavor with a peppery quality.

COLLARD GREENS The large, thick, smooth leaves of collard greens are a favorite of cooks in the American South. They have a mild flavor, but their tough texture requires a little more cooking time than other greens.

CORIANDER, GROUND Made from the dried ripe fruit of fresh coriander, or cilantro, this spice gives dishes an exotic taste. Its flavor is said to be like a combination of lemon, sage, and caraway.

CREAM, HEAVY Often labeled "heavy whipping cream" and also known as double cream, heavy cream has a high percentage of milk fat, which gives it a rich flavor.

CRÈME FRAÎCHE A soured cultured cream product, originally from France, crème fraîche is similar to sour cream but richer and subtler in flavor. When added to a sauce, it won't curdle or separate.

CUMIN This spice comes from the seeds of a member of the parsley family and has a distinct aroma and a nutty, smoky flavor.

CURRY POWDER Typical ingredients in this ground spice blend from South Asia include turmeric, cumin, coriander, pepper, cardamom, mustard, cloves, and ginger. Curry powders are categorized as mild, hot, and very hot. Madras curry powder is a well-balanced version with medium heat.

EGGPLANT The most familiar eggplant, called a globe eggplant, is usually large and has thin, shiny, deep purple skin that looks almost black. Asian eggplants, also purple skinned (either pale or deep), are smaller, longer, and narrower. Both types have mild, meaty flesh. Choose eggplants, also known as aubergines, that are firm and glossy.

FENNEL The stems of the fennel plant swell to overlap at the base, forming a bulb with white to pale green ribbed layers that look similar to celery. The green fronds are light and feathery. Fennel has a sweet anise flavor.

GINGER A refreshing combination of spicy and sweet in aroma and flavor, ginger adds a lively note to many recipes. Although often called a root, ginger is actually a rhizome, or underground stem. Select ginger that is firm and heavy, with smooth, unbroken skin.

HERBS
Using fresh herbs is one of the best things you can do to improve your cooking. Dried herbs do have their place, but fresh herbs usually bring brighter flavors to a dish.

Basil Used throughout the Mediterranean and in Southeast Asia, fresh basil is highly aromatic with a sweet, aniselike taste.

Bay These elongated gray-green leaves are often used to season braising liquids, imparting a slightly sweet, citrusy, nutty flavor. They are most often sold dried.

Chervil A delicate springtime herb with a taste reminiscent of parsley and anise.

Chives These slender, hollow, grasslike blades are used to give an onionlike flavor to dishes, without the pungent bite.

Cilantro Also called fresh coriander or Chinese parsley, cilantro has a bright astringent taste.

Marjoram A Mediterranean native, this herb has a milder, sweeter flavor than its cousin, oregano. It is used fresh or dried.

Mint This bright-tasting herb is available in many types, with spearmint the most commonly found variety.

Oregano One of the few herbs that keeps its flavor when dried, oregano, also known as wild marjoram, is spicy and aromatic.

Parsley, flat-leaf This dark green Italian variety of the clean, bracing herb adds vibrant color and pleasing flavor.

Rosemary Woody rosemary has leaves like pine needles and an assertive flavor.

Sage These soft, gray-green leaves are highly perfumed and have a pungent flavor with sweet tones. They are best used fresh.

Tarragon The slender, deep green leaves and elegant, aniselike scent of this herb make it particularly popular with French cooks.

Thyme Tiny green leaves on thin stems, this herb is a mild, all-purpose seasoning with a floral, earthy flavor. It is used fresh or dried.

JALAPEÑO CHILE This fresh hot chile measures 2–4 inches (5–10 cm) long and ranges from mildly hot to fiery. To reduce the heat, remove the ribs and seeds.

LEEK A mild-flavored member of the onion family, a leek is long and cylindrical, with a pale white root end and dark green leaves.

MACE Usually sold ground, mace is the dried bright red, lacy membrane that covers the nutmeg seed. Its flavor is a deeper and more pungent version of nutmeg.

MIRIN An important ingredient in Japanese cuisine, mirin is a sweet cooking wine made by fermenting glutinous rice and sugar.

MUSHROOMS
Thousands of mushroom varieties exist in the world, but only a fraction of them make it to the table, where they are enjoyed for their rich, earthy flavor. These are some of the more common varieties.

Button This small, round mushroom is the one most commonly stocked in markets.

Cremini Also known as Italian or Roman mushrooms or common brown mushrooms, cremini mature to become portobellos.

Morel This wild mushroom has an intense musky flavor, an elongated, spongelike cap, and a hollow stem. Morels are also dried.

Oyster Cream to pale gray, oyster mushrooms have a fan shape and a subtle flavor. Look for small, young mushrooms, as they become tough and bitter as they age.

Porcini Also called ceps, porcini have a sweet fragrance and full, earthy taste. They are rarely found fresh, so many recipes call for dried porcini.

Portobello The mature form of cremini mushrooms, with caps about 6 inches (15 cm) wide, a rich flavor, and a meaty texture.

MUSTARD

At its simplest, prepared mustard is a mixture of ground mustard seed and water. But this basic paste has been refined around the world by adding a number of flavorful ingredients.

Dijon Originating in Dijon, France, this silky smooth and slightly tangy mustard contains white wine and herbs.

Whole-grain The seeds of this mustard have been left mostly whole, giving it a pleasant, rustic texture.

NONREACTIVE A term used to describe a pan, dish, or bowl made of or lined with a material that will not react with acidic ingredients. This includes stainless steel, enamel, ceramic, and glass.

OIL

Cooking oils play an essential role in the kitchen. The other ingredients and the heat requirements of a recipe usually suggest which oil is most appropriate to use. Choose less refined, more flavorful oils for seasoning, and refined, less flavorful oils for cooking.

Asian sesame Pressed from toasted sesame seeds, this deep amber–colored oil has a rich, nutty flavor. The oil is best when it is used as a seasoning.

Canola This neutral-flavored oil, notable for its monounsaturated fats, is recommended for general cooking.

Grapeseed Pressed from grape seeds and mild in flavor, this oil heats to very high temperatures without smoking.

Olive This essential ingredient throughout the Mediterranean contributes a delicate, fruity taste to dishes. Full-flavored extra-virgin olive oil is produced from the first pressing of the olives without the use of heat or chemicals. The finest extra-virgin oils are clear green or golden, have a fruity, slightly peppery flavor, and are used to best advantage when they are not cooked. Olive oils extracted using heat or chemicals, then filtered and blended may be used for general cooking. In the past, such oils were labeled "pure olive oil." Today, they are simply labeled "olive oil." Lighter, less costly extra-virgin olive oils may be used for general cooking as well.

Peanut With a hint of rich flavor that comes from the peanuts pressed to make it, peanut oil is a popular choice for stir-frying.

ONIONS

This humble bulb vegetable, in the same family as leeks and garlic, is one of the most common ingredients in the kitchen.

Boiling These onions are small and have a mild flavor. They are somewhat larger than pearl onions and are delicious when roasted.

Green Also known as scallions or spring onions, green onions are the immature shoots of the bulb onion, with a narrow, white base; long, flat green leaves; and a mild flavor.

Pearl Sweeter than full-sized onions, pearl onions are no more than 1 inch (2.5 cm) in diameter, with papery skins. They hold their color and shape well when cooked.

Red These onions tend to be mild, slightly sweet, and purplish.

Red onion shoot Also called red scallions, these onions are similar to green onions, with a reddish base.

Yellow This common, all-purpose onion is usually too harsh for serving raw, but becomes rich and sweet when cooked.

PAPRIKA Red or orange-red, paprika is ground from dried peppers (capsicums). The finest paprikas available come from Hungary and Spain in three basic grades: sweet, medium-sweet, and hot.

PARSNIP A relative of the carrot, this ivory-colored root closely resembles its brighter, more familiar cousin. Parsnips have a sweet flavor and a tough, starchy texture that softens with cooking.

PEAS

The pea is one of the major groups of the large legume family. There are two general categories of the group eaten fresh: peas that are shelled and pod peas. In both cases, look for smooth, crisp green pods.

English This is the most common type of pea for shelling. Always make sure the peas are as bright and green as the pods. Yellowing peas and dull pods indicate the peas are turning starchy.

Snow Also called mangetouts, these flat, wide, bright green peas are eaten pod and all and often star in stir-fries.

Sugar snap Plumper and rounder than snow peas, this pod pea is also used in stir-fries.

PINE NUTS These nuts are actually seeds harvested from the cones of certain varieties of pine. Small, rich, and pale gold in color, they have an elongated, slightly tapered shape and a resinous, sweet flavor.

POLENTA Coarsely ground cornmeal that is cooked in either water or stock until it thickens and becomes tender.

POTATOES

Different varieties of potato have different starch levels, making some a better match for certain cooking methods than others. High-starch potatoes with dry, fluffy flesh such as russets are best for baking or mashing. Waxy, low-starch types, such as new potatoes, fingerlings, or red potatoes, hold their shape well when cooked and are ideal for boiling or roasting. Medium-starch varieties, also called all-purpose potatoes, have some of the characteristics of both types and are well-suited for many methods. Yukon golds are among the best known.

Fingerling Small, narrow, and knobby, fingerlings come in a variety of colors and are low in starch.

New These immature potatoes, usually a round red or white variety, are harvested in spring and summer. They have thin, papery skins and a short shelf life.

Red Also known as boiling potatoes, these round potatoes have thin, red skins, waxy flesh, and a dense, moist texture.

Russet These large, oval potatoes have dry, reddish brown skin and starchy flesh that is perfect for mashing. They are also known as baking or Idaho potatoes.

Yukon gold Thin-skinned potatoes with yellowish skin and golden, fine-grained, buttery-tasting flesh.

RED PEPPER FLAKES The flakes and seeds that result from crushing dried red chiles. Just a pinch or two of the flakes will add a bit of heat to a recipe.

RUTABAGA This member of the cabbage family looks like an overgrown turnip, to which it is closely related. Rutabagas come in a variety of colors, with skin that ranges in gradations of brown to yellow to violet. Their firm, yellow-orange flesh has a strong mustardlike taste that mellows and becomes sweeter when cooked.

SALT, SEA Available in coarse or fine grains, this salt is produced naturally by evaporation. The taste of each variety is influenced by where it was harvested. The grains are hollow, flaky pyramids, which dissolve more readily than regular table salt and add texture when sprinkled over a dish.

SEEDS
Seeds play an important part in any spice pantry. Whether used whole or freshly ground, they add flavor, aroma, and texture.

Caraway A member of the parsley family, caraway seeds have a strong, pungent taste that is closely identified with rye bread.

Fennel These elongated striped seeds have an aniselike flavor.

Sesame Tiny and flat, these seeds range in color from white to tan to black. They are often toasted before using.

SHALLOTS These small members of the onion family look like large cloves of garlic covered with papery bronze skin. Shallots have white flesh streaked with purple and a flavor more subtle than that of onions.

SHAOXING WINE A type of Chinese rice wine, yellow-gold Shaoxing wine adds flavor to sauces and stir-fries.

SHERRY, DRY This fortified wine, originally from Spain, is often used in cooking. It has a mellow, nutty flavor.

SQUASHES, SUMMER
All squashes are members of the gourd family but are divided into two branches: summer squash and winter squash. Summer squashes are best when young and fresh. Look for smaller squashes for the most tender bite.

Crookneck This bright yellow squash is similar in size to a zucchini (courgette), but with a curved neck and bulbous end. Younger, smaller squashes are more uniform.

Zucchini The best-known member of the summer squash family, most zucchini are long, narrow, and green. However, pale green to green-black varieties, ridged Italian heirlooms, and bright yellow zucchini are also available.

SQUASHES, WINTER
The members of this branch of the squash clan are allowed to mature until their flesh is thick and their shells are hard. Their dense flesh takes considerable time to steam or bake but yields tender, sweet results.

Blue hubbard These large squash have bright orange flesh and pale gray-blue skin with small bumps. They are excellent puréed.

Butternut This large squash has smooth beige skin and orange-yellow flesh. It is identifiable by the round bulb at the blossom end.

Delicata Generally small, delicata squashes are about 7 inches (18 cm) long and weigh about ½ pound (250 g). As its name suggests, this squash has a delicate rather than meaty flavor.

Kabocha Sweet and fine textured, the globe-shaped kabocha has pale-orange flesh and striated green skin.

STOCK, CHICKEN A liquid derived from slowly simmering chicken along with herbs and aromatic ingredients such as onions in water. Stock can be made at home and frozen for future use or purchased at better markets. Good-quality canned broths are available, but they tend to be saltier than homemade stock. Seek out brands labeled "low-sodium" or "reduced-sodium," so you can better control the seasonings in your dishes.

SWEET POTATOES Two types of sweet potatoes are commonly found: one with yellow-brown skin and yellow flesh, and one with dark reddish or purplish skin and dark orange flesh. The latter is sometimes called a yam in the United States, although it is botanically unrelated to the true yam, which is a tropical tuber. Choose firm, unblemished sweet potatoes with no breaks in their thin skin.

TURNIP The common turnip is a root vegetable with crisp, white flesh and white skin with a purple cap, although some varieties have yellow flesh and the cap might be green, red, white, or even black. Young turnips are tender and have a mild, sweet flavor. The flavor grows stronger and the flesh woodier with age.

VINEGAR
Many types of vinegar are available, made from various red or white wines or, like cider and rice vinegars, from fruits and grains.

Balsamic Made from the unfermented grape juice of white Trebbiano grapes, balsamic may be aged briefly, for only 1 year, or for as long as 75 years. The vinegar evaporates and grows sweeter and mellower with time.

Cider A fruity vinegar made from apples and used in many traditional American recipes. Try an organic, unrefined cider vinegar if you can find one.

Red wine A pantry staple, red wine vinegar is made when red wine is allowed to ferment naturally over a period of months. Seek out vinegar that has been aged for the best quality.

Rice Produced from fermented rice, this vinegar adds a slight acidity to dishes. It is available unseasoned or sweetened; the latter is labeled "seasoned rice vinegar."

Sherry This full-bodied vinegar, originally from Spain, has a full, nutty taste.

WAX BEANS Long beans with the same characteristics as green beans, but pale or medium yellow in color.

WHITE PEPPER This variety of pepper is made from black peppercorns that have had their skins removed before the berries are dried. White pepper is often less aromatic and milder than black pepper. It is favored in the preparation of light-colored dishes.

WINE, WHITE Cooking with white wine adds acidity and flavor. Any type you have on hand is fine. Sauvignon Blanc or Pinot Grigio would both be fine choices.

ZEST The colored portion of citrus peel, which is rich in flavorful oils. The white portion of the peel, called the pith, is bitter. Choose organic citrus fruits for zesting, since pesticides concentrate in the thin skins.

Index

A

Apples, Red Cabbage Braised with Bacon
   and, 80
ARTICHOKES
   about, 136
   Braised Artichokes with Shallots and
     Peas, 65–69
   Roasted Baby Artichokes, 118
ASPARAGUS
   about, 136
   Asparagus with Fresh Herbs, 97
   Basic Sautéed Vegetables, 24–25
   Roasted Asparagus with Orange-Shallot
     Butter, 131
   Stir-fried Spring Vegetables with Ginger,
     Lemon, and Mint, 89–93

B

Baby Bok Choy with Sesame Oil, 56
BACON
   Black Kale with Red Onion and Bacon, 101
   Braised Brussels Sprouts with Bacon and
     Onion, 84
   dicing, 37
   Red Cabbage Braised with Bacon and
     Apples, 80
BAKING
   about, 16, 104
   Butternut Squash Gratin, 129
   Classic Potato Gratin, 126–28
   equipment for, 133
   Fennel and Potato Gratin, 129
   Summer Squash Tian, 121–25
   Sweet Potato Gratin, 129
   Tomatoes Stuffed with Rice, Basil, and
     Cheese, 107–11
Basic Braised Vegetables, 22–23
Basic Roasted Vegetables, 26–27
Basic Sautéed Vegetables, 24–25
Basic Steamed Vegetables, 20–21
BASIL
   about, 137
   Mashed Potatoes with Basil Purée, 52
   Pesto, 59
   Tomatoes Stuffed with Rice, Basil, and
     Cheese, 107–11
Bay leaves, 137
BEANS
   about, 136, 139
   Green Beans and Yellow Wax Beans with
     Pesto, 59

BEETS
   about, 136
   Beets Glazed with Honey, Orange, and
     Clove, 77
   Beets with Salsa Verde, 57
   Roasted Winter Root Vegetables with
     Rosemary, 113–17
BELGIAN ENDIVE
   about, 136
   Endives with Cream Sauce, 73
BELL PEPPERS
   about, 136
   Basic Sautéed Vegetables, 24–25
   Sautéed Peppers and Onion, 95–96
   stuffing, 111
BLACK KALE
   about, 136
   Black Kale with Red Onion and Bacon, 101
BOILING
   about, 15, 44
   Buttermilk Mashed Potatoes with Goat
     Cheese, 52
   Classic Mashed Potatoes, 47–51
   Corn on the Cob with Chile-Lime Butter, 60
   equipment for, 132
   Green Beans and Yellow Wax Beans with
     Pesto, 59
   Mashed Potatoes and Celery Root, 53
   Mashed Potatoes with Basil Purée, 52
   Mashed Potatoes with Cabbage and Green
     Onions, 53
   Mashed Potatoes with Olive Oil and Garlic, 52
   Mashed Yukon Gold Potatoes and Turnips, 53
BOK CHOY, BABY
   about, 136
   Baby Bok Choy with Sesame Oil, 56
BRAISING
   about, 15, 62
   Basic Braised Vegetables, 22–23
   Beets Glazed with Honey, Orange, and
     Clove, 77
   Braised Artichokes with Shallots and
     Peas, 65–69
   Braised Brussels Sprouts with Bacon and
     Onion, 84
   Braised Fennel with White Wine and
     Tomato, 70–72
   Braised Mushrooms with Sherry and Cream, 83
   Celery with Lemon and Thyme, 73
   Endives with Cream Sauce, 73
   equipment for, 132–33

   Glazed Pearl Onions with Rosemary, 77
   Leeks with Mustard Sauce, 73
   Maple-Glazed Carrots with Shallots and
     Parsley, 75–76
   Mustard-Glazed Parsnips, 77
   Quick Braise of Spring Peas with Red Onion
     Shoots, 79
   Red Cabbage Braised with Bacon and
     Apples, 80
BREAD CRUMBS, FRESH
   about, 136
   making, 37
BROCCOLI
   Basic Steamed Vegetables, 20–21
   peeling and steaming stalks of, 54
   Steamed Broccoli with Lemon and Olive Oil, 54
   trimming, 38
BROCCOLI RABE
   about, 136
   Broccoli Rabe with Red Pepper and Garlic, 100
Brushes, 135
BRUSSELS SPROUTS
   about, 136
   Basic Steamed Vegetables, 20–21
   Braised Brussels Sprouts with Bacon and
     Onion, 84
   Brussels Sprouts and Onion with Oregano, 101
   preparing, 42
BUTTER
   about, 17
   Chile-Lime Butter, 60
   Curry Butter, 56
   Orange-Shallot Butter, 131
   Sage and Pecan Butter, 57
   Spicy Red Butter, 119
   unsalted, 136
BUTTERMILK
   about, 136
   Buttermilk Mashed Potatoes with Goat
     Cheese, 52
BUTTERNUT SQUASH
   about, 139
   Butternut Squash Gratin, 129

C

CABBAGE
   about, 9, 136
   Cabbage with Caraway Seeds and Sour
     Cream, 57
   Mashed Potatoes with Cabbage and Green
     Onions, 53

Red Cabbage Braised with Bacon and
    Apples, 80
working with, 39
Canola oil, 138
Capers, 136
CARROTS
    Basic Roasted Vegetables, 26–27
    Maple-Glazed Carrots with Shallots and
        Parsley, 75–76
    Roasted Whole Carrots with Shallots and
        Herbs, 118
    Roasted Winter Root Vegetables with
        Rosemary, 113–17
CAULIFLOWER
    Basic Steamed Vegetables, 20–21
    Cauliflower with Curry Butter, 56
    peeling and steaming stems of, 54
    trimming, 39
Cayenne, 136
CELERY
    Basic Braised Vegetables, 22–23
    Celery with Lemon and Thyme, 73
CELERY ROOT
    about, 136
    Mashed Potatoes and Celery Root, 53
    working with, 42
CHARD
    about, 136
    Chard with Lemon, 100
CHEESE
    about, 136
    Buttermilk Mashed Potatoes with Goat
        Cheese, 52
    Butternut Squash Gratin, 129
    Classic Potato Gratin, 126–28
    Tomatoes Stuffed with Rice, Basil, and
        Cheese, 107–11
Chervil, 137
CHILES
    Chile-Lime Butter, 60
    chipotle, 137
    jalapeño, 137
    working with, 33
CHIVES
    about, 137
    snipping, 34
Cilantro, 137
CITRUS FRUITS. *See also individual fruits*
    seasoning with, 17
    zesting and juicing, 38
Classic Mashed Potatoes, 47–51
Classic Potato Gratin, 126–28
Cloves, 137
Coffee mills, 134
Colanders, 135

COLLARD GREENS
    about, 137
    Slivered Collards with Toasted Sesame
        Seeds, 100
Coriander, 137
CORN
    Corn on the Cob with Chile-Lime Butter, 60
    grilling, 60
Cream, heavy, 137
Creamed Spinach with Basil, 101
Crème fraîche, 137
Cumin, 137
Curry Butter, 56
Curry powder, 137
Cutting boards, 134

D
DELICATA SQUASH
    about, 139
    Roasted Delicata Squash with Spicy Red
        Butter, 119
Dutch ovens, 133

E
EGGPLANT
    about, 137
    salting, 103
    Stir-fried Sesame Eggplant, 103
    stuffing, 111
Endive. *See* Belgian endive
Equipment, 132–35

F
FENNEL
    about, 137
    Basic Braised Vegetables, 22–23
    Braised Fennel with White Wine and
        Tomato, 70–72
    Fennel and Potato Gratin, 129
    Sautéed Fennel, 97
    working with, 41
Food processors, 134
Frying pans, 133

G
Garlic, 32
Garnishing, 17
Ginger, 137
Glazed Pearl Onions with Rosemary, 77
Grapeseed oil, 138
Graters, 134
GRATINS
    Butternut Squash Gratin, 129
    Classic Potato Gratin, 126–28

Fennel and Potato Gratin, 129
    Sweet Potato Gratin, 129
Green Beans and Yellow Wax Beans with
    Pesto, 59
GREEN ONIONS
    about, 138
    Mashed Potatoes with Cabbage and Green
        Onions, 53
    working with, 33
GREENS. *See also individual greens*
    about, 9
    rinsing, 40, 98
    sautéing, 100–101
    stemming, 40
Grinding, 134

H
HERBS. *See also individual herbs*
    about, 137
    seasoning with, 17
    working with, 34–36

J
Juicing, 38, 134

K
Knives, 15, 134

L
LEEKS
    about, 137
    Basic Braised Vegetables, 22–23
    Fennel and Potato Gratin, 129
    Leeks with Mustard Sauce, 73
LEMONS
    Celery with Lemon and Thyme, 73
    Chard with Lemon, 100
    juicing, 38
    Sautéed Spinach with Garlic and Lemon, 98
    Steamed Broccoli with Lemon and Olive
        Oil, 54
    Stir-fried Spring Vegetables with Ginger,
        Lemon, and Mint, 89–93
    zesting, 38
LIMES
    Chile-Lime Butter, 60
    juicing, 38
    zesting, 38
Linens, 135

M
Mace, 137
Mandolines, 134

Maple-Glazed Carrots with Shallots and
    Parsley, 75–76
Marjoram, 137
Mashed Potatoes and Celery Root, 53
Mashed Potatoes with Basil Purée, 52
Mashed Potatoes with Cabbage and Green
    Onions, 53
Mashed Potatoes with Olive Oil and Garlic, 52
Mashed Potato Pancakes, 51
Mashed Yukon Gold Potatoes and Turnips, 53
Mashers, 135
MEASURING
    tips for, 14, 75
    tools for, 134
Mint, 137
Mirin, 137
Mise en place, 14
Mixing bowls, 134
Mortar and pestle, 134–35
MUSHROOMS
    about, 10, 137
    Braised Mushrooms with Sherry and
        Cream, 83
    preparing, 43
MUSTARD
    about, 138
    Mustard-Glazed Parsnips, 77
    Mustard Sauce, 73

N

New Potatoes with Butter, Shallot, and
    Tarragon, 56
Nonreactive cookware, 138
Nuts, toasting, 36

O

Oil, 17, 138
ONIONS. See also Green onions; Onion shoots
    about, 11, 138
    Black Kale with Red Onion and Bacon, 101
    Braised Brussel Sprouts with Bacon and Onion, 84
    dicing, 30
    Glazed Pearl Onions with Rosemary, 77
    Roasted Winter Root Vegetables with
        Rosemary, 113–17
    Sautéed Peppers and Onion, 95–96
    Summer Squash Tian, 121–25
ONION SHOOTS
    about, 138
    Quick Braise of Spring Peas with Red Onion
        Shoots, 79
ORANGES
    Beets Glazed with Honey, Orange, and
        Clove, 77

juicing, 38
    Orange-Shallot Butter, 131
    zesting, 38
Oregano, 137
Organic vegetables, 11
Oven mitts, 135

P

Pancakes, Mashed Potato, 51
Pans, 132–33
Paprika, 138
Parsley, 137
PARSNIPS
    about, 138
    Mustard-Glazed Parsnips, 77
    Roasted Winter Root Vegetables with
        Rosemary, 113–17
Pastry brushes, 135
Peanut oil, 138
PEAS
    about, 138
    Braised Artichokes with Shallots and
        Peas, 65–69
    Quick Braise of Spring Peas with Red Onion
        Shoots, 79
    Stir-fried Spring Vegetables with Ginger,
        Lemon, and Mint, 89–93
Pecan and Sage Butter, 57
Peelers, 134
Pepper mills, 135
Pesto, 59
Pine nuts, 138
Polenta, 138
POTATOES
    about, 138
    Basic Roasted Vegetables, 26–27
    Buttermilk Mashed Potatoes with Goat
        Cheese, 52
    Classic Mashed Potatoes, 47–51
    Classic Potato Gratin, 126–28
    Fennel and Potato Gratin, 129
    Mashed Potatoes and Celery Root, 53
    Mashed Potatoes with Basil Purée, 52
    Mashed Potatoes with Cabbage and Green
        Onions, 53
    Mashed Potatoes with Olive Oil and
        Garlic, 52
    Mashed Potato Pancakes, 51
    Mashed Yukon Gold Potatoes and Turnips, 53
    New Potatoes with Butter, Shallot, and
        Tarragon, 56
    Roasted Potato Wedges, 119
    Roasted Winter Root Vegetables with
        Rosemary, 113–17

Smashed Potatoes, 51
    working with, 42
Potholders, 135
Pots, 132–33

Q

Quick Braise of Spring Peas with Red Onion
    Shoots, 79

R

Red Cabbage Braised with Bacon and Apples, 80
Red pepper flakes, 138
Rice, Tomatoes Stuffed with Basil, Cheese,
    and, 107–11
Ricers, 135
ROASTING
    about, 16, 104
    Basic Roasted Vegetables, 26–27
    equipment for, 133
    Roasted Asparagus with Orange-Shallot
        Butter, 131
    Roasted Baby Artichokes, 118
    Roasted Cherry Tomatoes, 118
    Roasted Delicata Squash with Spicy Red
        Butter, 119
    Roasted Potato Wedges, 119
    Roasted Sweet Potatoes with Soy Glaze, 119
    Roasted Whole Carrots with Shallots and
        Herbs, 118
    Roasted Winter Root Vegetables with
        Rosemary, 113–17
ROSEMARY
    about, 137
    Roasted Winter Root Vegetables with
        Rosemary, 113–17
    working with, 35
RUTABAGAS
    about, 139
    Roasted Winter Root Vegetables with
        Rosemary, 113–17
    working with, 42

S

SAGE
    about, 137
    Sage and Pecan Butter, 57
Salsa Verde, 57
Salt, 16–17, 139
Saucepans, 132
SAUCES
    Mustard Sauce, 73
    Pesto, 59
SAUTÉING
    about, 16, 86

Asparagus with Fresh Herbs, 97
Basic Sautéed Vegetables, 24–25
Black Kale with Red Onion and Bacon, 101
Broccoli Rabe with Red Pepper and
    Garlic, 100
Brussels Sprouts and Onion with
    Oregano, 101
Chard with Lemon, 100
Creamed Spinach with Basil, 101
equipment for, 133
Sautéed Fennel, 97
Sautéed Peppers and Onion, 95–96
Sautéed Spinach with Garlic and Lemon, 98
Slivered Collards with Toasted Sesame
    Seeds, 100
Zucchini with Toasted Bread Crumbs, 97
Scissors, 135
Seasoning, 16–17
Seasons, 12–13
SEEDS
    about, 139
    toasting, 36
Serving, 17, 135
Sesame oil, Asian, 138
SHALLOTS
    about, 139
    Braised Artichokes with Shallots and
        Peas, 65–69
    dicing, 31
    Maple-Glazed Carrots with Shallots and
        Parsley, 75–76
    Orange-Shallot Butter, 131
    Roasted Whole Carrots with Shallots and
        Herbs, 118
Sherry, 139
Shredders, 134
Sieves, 135
Skillets, 133
Skimmers, 135
Slicers, 134
Slivered Collards with Toasted Sesame
    Seeds, 100
Smashed Potatoes, 51
Spatulas, 135
Spicy Red Butter, 119
SPINACH
    Creamed Spinach with Basil, 101
    rinsing and drying, 98
    Sautéed Spinach with Garlic and Lemon, 98
Spinners, 135
SPOONS
    measuring, 134
    metal, 135
    wooden, 135
Squash. See Summer squash; Winter squash

STEAMING
    about, 15, 44
    Baby Bok Choy with Sesame Oil, 56
    Basic Steamed Vegetables, 20–21
    Beets with Salsa Verde, 57
    Cabbage with Caraway Seeds and Sour
        Cream, 57
    Cauliflower with Curry Butter, 56
    equipment for, 132
    New Potatoes with Butter, Shallot, and
        Tarragon, 56
    Steamed Broccoli with Lemon and
        Olive Oil, 54
    Winter Squash with Sage and Pecan Butter, 57
STIR-FRYING
    about, 16, 86
    equipment for, 133
    Stir-fried Sesame Eggplant, 103
    Stir-fried Spring Vegetables with Ginger,
        Lemon, and Mint, 89–93
Stock, chicken, 139
Stockpots, 132
SUMMER SQUASH
    about, 11, 139
    Basic Sautéed Vegetables, 24–25
    stuffing, 111
    Summer Squash Tian, 121–25
    Zucchini with Toasted Bread Crumbs, 97
SWEET POTATOES
    about, 139
    Basic Roasted Vegetables, 26–27
    Roasted Sweet Potatoes with Soy Glaze, 119
    Sweet Potato Gratin, 129
Swiss chard. See Chard

T
Tarragon, 137
Thyme, 137
Tian, Summer Squash, 121–25
TOMATOES
    Braised Fennel with White Wine and
        Tomato, 70–72
    Roasted Cherry Tomatoes, 118
    storing, 110
    Tomatoes Stuffed with Rice, Basil, and
        Cheese, 107–11
    varieties of, 109
Tongs, 135
Tools, 132–35
Towels, 135
TURNIPS
    about, 139
    Mashed Yukon Gold Potatoes and
        Turnips, 53

V
VEGETABLES. See also individual vegetables
    Basic Braised Vegetables, 22–23
    Basic Roasted Vegetables, 26–27
    Basic Sautéed Vegetables, 24–25
    Basic Steamed Vegetables, 20–21
    cleaning, 23
    cooking methods for, 14–16
    garnishing, 17
    measuring, 14
    organic, 11
    peeling, 14
    rinsing, 14
    seasoning, 16–17
    seasons for, 12–13
    serving, 17
    types of, 9–11
    working with round, 42
Vinegar, 139

W
Whisks, 135
White pepper, 139
WINE
    Shaoxing, 139
    white, 139
WINTER SQUASH
    about, 11, 139
    Butternut Squash Gratin, 129
    preparing, 43
    Roasted Delicata Squash with Spicy Red
        Butter, 119
    Winter Squash with Sage and Pecan
        Butter, 57
Woks, 133

Z
Zest, 38, 139
ZUCCHINI
    about, 139
    Basic Sautéed Vegetables, 24–25
    Summer Squash Tian, 121–25
    Zucchini with Toasted Bread Crumbs, 97

FREE PRESS

A Division of Simon & Schuster, Inc.
1230 Avenue of the Americas
New York, NY 10020

WILLIAMS-SONOMA

Founder & Vice-Chairman Chuck Williams

WELDON OWEN INC.

Chief Executive Officer John Owen
President and Chief Operating Officer Terry Newell
Chief Financial Officer Christine E. Munson
Vice President International Sales Stuart Laurence
Creative Director Gaye Allen
Publisher Hannah Rahill
Senior Editor Jennifer Newens
Managing Editor Heather Belt
Associate Editors Donita Boles and Lauren Higgins
Art Director Kyrie Forbes
Designers Adrienne Aquino and Andrea Stephany
Production Director Chris Hemesath
Color Manager Teri Bell
Production and Reprint Coordinator Todd Rechner
Food Stylist Alison Attenborough
Prop Stylist Leigh Nöe
Assistant Food Stylists Katie Christ, Jeffrey Larsen, and Jen Carden
Assistant Food Stylist and Hand Model Abby Whitridge

PHOTO CREDITS

Tucker & Hossler, all photography, except the following:
Bill Bettencourt: pages 32, 33 (jalapeño chile sequence),
36 (nuts & seeds sequence), and 37 (bacon sequence);
Mark Thomas: pages 30, 31, and 38 (citrus sequence).

THE MASTERING SERIES

Conceived and produced by Weldon Owen Inc.
814 Montgomery Street, San Francisco, CA 94133
Telephone: 415 291 0100 Fax: 415 291 8841

In collaboration with Williams-Sonoma, Inc.
3250 Van Ness Avenue, San Francisco, CA 94109

A WELDON OWEN PRODUCTION
Copyright © 2006 by Weldon Owen Inc. and Williams-Sonoma Inc.

All rights reserved, including the right of reproduction in whole or in part
in any form.

FREE PRESS and colophon are registered trademarks of Simon & Schuster, Inc.

For information regarding special discounts for bulk purchases,
please contact Simon & Schuster Special Sales at 1 800 456 6798 or
business@simonandschuster.com

Set in ITC Berkeley and FF The Sans.

Color separations by Embassy Graphics.
Printed and bound in China by SNP Leefung Printers Limited.

First printed in 2006.

10 9 8 7 6 5 4 3 2 1

Library of Congress Cataloging-in-Publication data is available.

ISBN–13: 978-0-7432-8439-4
ISBN–10: 0-7432-8439-9

ACKNOWLEDGMENTS

Weldon Owen wishes to thank the following people for their
generous support in producing this book: Desne Ahlers, Carrie Bradley,
Ken DellaPenta, Lesli Neilson, Sharon Silva, Bob Simmons, and
Coleen Simmons.

A NOTE ON WEIGHTS AND MEASURES

All recipes include customary U.S. and metric measurements. Metric conversions are based on
a standard developed for these books and have been rounded off. Actual weights may vary.